WHY CATHOLICS LEAVE,
WHAT THEY MISS,
AND
HOW THEY
MIGHT RETURN

WHY CATHOLICS LEAVE, WHAT THEY MISS, AND HOW THEY MIGHT RETURN

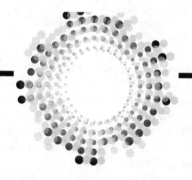

Stephen Bullivant, Catherine Knowles,
Hannah Vaughan-Spruce, and
Bernadette Durcan

With contributions from Sherry Weddell,
Fr. James Mallon, and Rt. Rev. Philip Egan

Paulist Press
New York / Mahwah, NJ

Cover image courtesy publicdomainvectors.org
Cover and book design by Sharyn Banks

Library of Congress Cataloging-in-Publication Data

Names: Bullivant, Stephen Sebastian, 1984– author.
Title: Why Catholics leave, what they miss, and how they might return / Stephen Bullivant, Catherine Knowles, Hannah Vaughan-Spruce, and Bernadette Durcan.
Description: New York : Paulist Press, 2019. | Includes bibliographical references.
Identifiers: LCCN 2018018815 (print) | LCCN 2018041643 (ebook) | ISBN 9781587687860 (ebook) | ISBN 9780809154098 (pbk. : alk. paper)
Subjects: LCSH: Ex-church members—Catholic Church. | Catholic Church—Membership. | Church attendance.
Classification: LCC BX2347.8.E82 (ebook) | LCC BX2347.8.E82 W49 2019 (print) | DDC 282—dc23
LC record available at https://lccn.loc.gov/2018018815

ISBN 978-0-8091-5409-8 (paperback)
ISBN 978-1-58768-786-0 (e-book)

Published by Paulist Press
997 Macarthur Boulevard
Mahwah, New Jersey 07430

www.paulistpress.com

Printed and bound in the
United States of America

With thanks to all those who took the trouble to
"share their story" with us

CONTENTS

FOREWORD

Since becoming a priest, I have been greatly concerned about "lapsed" Catholics: how to reach out to them, how to help them become more enthusiastic disciples, and how to draw them into a deeper relationship with Christ and his Church. In the Diocese of Portsmouth, the Sunday attendance rate in 2017 was about 14 percent. In other words, more than eight out of every ten baptized Catholics never attend Sunday Mass except at perhaps Christmas. Why is this? Is there anything we can do? Most of them, having been baptized, have also made their first holy communion and received the sacrament of confirmation. Some pray regularly, while others have strong connections with the Church through the parish school or attending baptisms and funerals. We know many of them because they are loved ones, members of our own families; however, for each of them, something seems to be missing or misfiring. Why do they not wish for a deeper, life-changing communion with Jesus Christ in his sacraments? Do they realize what they are missing? I cannot claim to have had much success in drawing such people back, although prayer for the "lapsed" does form a key part of my daily prayers.

So, who are the lapsed? What do they think about the Church? Why do they not practice? We call them "lapsed," yet over the generations, many have never practiced, and so technically, they have not lapsed at all. They simply do not practice. Others have chosen to leave the fold. Some have drifted and might, with the right conditions, return. Is there anything we can do to attract any of these people back to the Church?

In autumn 2015, the diocese, in a fruitful and generous collaboration with St. Mary's University, Twickenham, launched an online survey called "Share Your Story" that was aimed at baptized nonpracticing Catholics. The survey invited them to share their reasons for leaving the Church. At the time, we wanted to hear from anyone who was a baptized Catholic and who did not regularly attend Mass or who no longer identified as Catholic. My hope was that the survey would be a means of enlightening our parishes and schools, our clergy and laity, about the challenges the Church faces in the contemporary world and, where appropriate and possible, to change our ecclesial culture to become more accommodating and welcoming. I hoped it would help us listen to and learn from the different experiences of everyone.

This book, *Why Catholics Leave, What They Miss, and How They Might Return*, contains the results of that survey. I am sure you will find it fascinating. We are indebted to Professor Stephen Bullivant, Dr. Catherine Knowles, Hannah Vaughan-Spruce, and Bernadette Durcan for collating, organizing, and interpreting the materials.

In our attempts as a diocese to move from maintenance to mission, we have been indebted to partners who have contributed their expertise. Sherry Weddell and the Catherine of Siena Institute helped us launch both the Called & Gifted™ Discernment process and Ananias training to equip lay Catholics in the Diocese of Portsmouth for evangelization. Fr. James Mallon of the Divine Renovation ministry, which helps parishes become more evangelizing, was the keynote speaker at our Clergy Convocation in June 2017. I am grateful to both Sherry Weddell and Fr. James Mallon for adding their own reflections to this book.

Through this study, may all of us who are practicing Catholics find new ways to reach out to and accompany our nonpracticing brothers and sisters on their journey of faith. This, in turn, will be an immense help to that new evangelization Saint John Paul II called for—an evangelization "new in its ardor, new in its methods and new in its expression."

+ Philip
Bishop of Portsmouth
The Solemnity of All Saints

PREFACE

SHERRY A. WEDDELL

The power of *Why Catholics Leave* is that the four authors sought out and really *listened in depth* to the stories of 256 nonpracticing and former Catholics associated with a single British diocese: Portsmouth. In doing so, they were listening for the "signs of the times" that come through the experiences of these people and were practicing a form of what Saint Pope John Paul II called "Gospel discernment":

> The Church has always had the duty of scrutinizing the signs of the times and of interpreting them in the light of the Gospel so that in a language intelligible to every generation, she can respond to the perennial questions which people ask about this present life and the life to come, and about the relationship of the one to the other. (*Pastores Dabo Vobis* 10)

One of the Catherine of Siena Institute's mantras in evangelization and disciple-making is "never accept a label in place of a story." I am sometimes regarded as the unofficial queen of unwelcome news since the first chapter of my book *Forming Intentional Disciples* was crammed with similar statistics and stories about the Catholic Church in the United States. But in fact, these stories are a source of genuine hope when understood through the lens of evangelization.

The reality is that everyone that you and I meet—practicing or former Catholic, Anglican, Quaker, Buddhist, or highly secular agnostic—is in spiritual motion. *Why Catholics Leave* makes it clear that (1) no Catholic just wakes up one morning and decides, "I think I'll become an atheist today"; (2) most former Catholics move away slowly in stages; and (3) most of these people return to personal faith and begin to follow Jesus as his disciples amid his Church the same way—in stages. What is also clear is that most potential returnees will require the active, personal assistance of local Catholics and Catholic communities to return.

It is especially important that, in addition to asking why Catholics stopped attending Mass or dropped their Catholic identity altogether, Stephen Bullivant and his team asked some brilliant, revealing questions: What did they miss, could they imagine themselves returning to the Church, and what specific things could the Church do to help?

The most surprising and hopeful findings in *Why Catholics Leave* for most Catholic leaders will probably be how many "leavers" still feel genuinely connected with the Church and Catholicism for several reasons. When working with clergy, I refer jokingly to these people as "half-a-Catholics," a term that my fellow catechumens and I called ourselves on our way into the Catholic Church.

This is not a unique phenomenon for the United Kingdom by any means. Recent studies have found that there are millions of people in the United States who feel "partially Catholic" even though they have left the Church and have even taken on new religious labels like Protestant or "nothing." We have also discovered that there is a hidden host of "partial Catholics" in the United States who were not raised as Catholics and did not even have Catholic parents. They grew up in different religious worlds altogether, and yet they still identify with Catholic values or practices in some meaningful way. Those felt connections are spiritual bridges across which twenty-first-century Catholic evangelizers can actively help people return to the Church or enter it for the first time.

I have seen tremendous growth in the Catholic world regarding evangelization over the past five years. Hundreds of parishes and now whole dioceses are embarking on the journey of moving from institutional maintenance to Evangelical mission in both the United Kingdom and the United States. The illuminating clarity that a book like *Why Catholics Leave* brings to the conversation is essential for Catholic leaders at this point in the life of the Church.

INTRODUCTION

Entire groups of the baptized have lost a living sense of the faith, or even no longer consider themselves members of the Church.

—Pope Saint John Paul II,
Redemptoris Missio (1990), no. 33

[We cannot] overlook the fact that in recent decades there has been a breakdown in the way Catholics pass down the Christian faith to the young. It is undeniable that many people feel disillusioned and no longer identify with the Catholic tradition.

—Pope Francis, *Evangelii Gaudium* (2013), no. 70

That a considerable proportion of Catholics no longer—and in some cases, perhaps never did—regularly practice the Faith into which they were baptized is not a secret. The website of our Bishop's Conference, for example, has for some years carried the estimate that there are "approximately four million" nonchurchgoing Catholics in England and Wales (CBCEW 2017). According to the recent *Contemporary Catholicism in England and Wales* report, using data from the 2012–14 waves of the British Social Attitudes survey, fewer than one in five cradle-Catholic adults say they now attend church weekly or more. Three out of every five, meanwhile, say that they attend never or practically never (Bullivant 2016a, 14). That equates to around 3.7 million people.

This report is the fruit of a project undertaken by a joint team from the Diocese of Portsmouth and the Benedict XVI Centre for Religion and Society at Saint Mary's University, Twickenham, with a very simple remit: to invite Catholics who no longer regularly practice their Faith to *share their story*, for these testimonies to be seriously listened to, and for what they have to say to be heard more widely. This plan embodies two hopes: first, that the Church might better discern in what ways it can serve those who are both missing and missed from our parishes; and second, that it might better understand the means of preventing others from leaving in the first place. As Bishop Philip Egan of Portsmouth wrote in his invitation for people to share their story:

> There are many people in Portsmouth and beyond, who were baptized Catholic but for one reason or another have lost interest in what the Catholic Church has to say. If you feel this way, then as the bishop, I'd love to hear from you!
>
> On the other hand, you may feel you are still interested and are attracted to the Church, but you don't have time for Sunday Mass. Or perhaps you find church boring, or your local parish unfriendly?
>
> Sadly, there are some who feel alienated from the Church because it has harmed or rejected them in some way. But again, if this is you, I'd love to hear from you!

To the best of our knowledge, this is the first time that a Catholic diocese in Britain has embarked upon such an exercise. Several of our respondents remarked upon the welcome novelty of being asked for their opinion. To quote just two: "I would like to thank you for offering this service for me to have my say" (female, 35); "I saw this survey and wanted to very much take part. Many thanks Bishop Philip for the opportunity to do so" (female, 65).

That said, this study is not the absolute first of its kind. In the late 1970s, the United States Conference of Catholic Bishops funded a major study of "religious change among Catholics," which included interviews with nearly two hundred Catholics who had recently ceased attending Mass (Hoge et al. 1981). In the late 1990s, funded by the Methodist Church, Philip Richter and Leslie Francis published a major study of British "church leavers" from a range of denominations, Catholics included; a follow-up study was published around a decade later (Richter and Francis 1998; Francis and Richter 2007). In 2007, the Australian Catholic Bishops Conference released a substantial report into "Catholics Who Have Stopped Attending Mass" (Dixon et al. 2007). More recently, and most germane to the present report, there have been a few Catholic-specific studies in the United States—most notably from the Dioceses of Trenton, New Jersey, and Springfield, Illinois, and researchers at New York's Fordham University—soliciting the testimonies of non- or irregularly practicing Catholics (see Byron and Zech 2012; Hardy et al. 2014; Beaudoin and Hornbeck 2013; Hornbeck 2013). These latter studies have deeply influenced our own, and we are grateful to their authors for their assistance.

OUR SAMPLE

The project took the form of a confidential web survey,[1] which was live from October 1 to December 31, 2015, at http://www .mystoryshared.co.uk (now defunct). This survey included both open-ended "write-in" questions, inviting participants to narrate their own stories, in their own words, and at whatever level of length or detail they felt appropriate, as well as a series of shorter, more specific questions deliberately replicating those asked in previous American diocesan surveys. A copy of the full survey is included as an appendix to this book. The invitation to participate in the survey was spread via social media, the national Catholic media, local media, parish newsletters, and word of mouth. We received just under three hundred responses, of which 256 were judged to meet our eligibility criteria.[2]

---

1. The survey was (and respondents were explicitly told that it was) anonymous, and no contact details for respondents were collected. At the end of the survey, respondents were given the opportunity to email if they were interested either in receiving updates on the survey's findings, or if they were willing for someone from the diocese's pastoral team to contact them. This was done, however, so that names and email addresses could not be directly correlated to a given response. Where respondents have given personal details—for example, names of places or private individuals—that could feasibly be used to identify them or any other person, we have been careful to remove these from our reporting (hence "parish X," etcetera, in some of the quoted excerpts).

2. At the gateway page to the web survey, potential respondents were informed of the following: "You are eligible to participate in this survey if you are (a) aged 18 years of age or older; (b) have been baptized as a Catholic; (c) either live or have lived within the Diocese of Portsmouth, and (d) no longer practice the Catholic faith (for whatever reason)." Although participants were required to affirm that they met these criteria, scrutiny of the responses revealed that in

A small set of background, demographic information was collected from our participants. This was deliberately kept minimal:
given the pastoral intent of the survey, we did not wish to ask
detailed information up front about such things as education, marital status, and sexuality, even though these might have been useful
for analytical purposes. While some background questions (sex,
age, race/ethnicity, religious affiliation, current religious practice)
were asked, we felt that limiting these would (a) aid completion
rates and (b) reduce risk of the exercise being perceived as a
bureaucratic, "form-filling" exercise. Instead, respondents clearly
felt comfortable in offering such details about their lives and back-
grounds when and where they felt that they were relevant to their
substantive responses later in the survey.

Of the respondents, 156 were female, 100 were male. The
mean age among the women was forty-seven (SD = fourteen), and
among the men forty-eight (SD = sixteen). Figure 1 presents a more
complete breakdown of the age/gender spread of our (eligible) survey respondents. Several things about the sample are worth noting.
The first is the large number of women, outnumbering men by a
ratio of three to one. Since other studies, using nationally representative datasets, show that levels of low and nonpractice are in fact
highest among Catholic men (e.g., Bullivant 2006b), it is evident
that women are overrepresented in our sample. The spread of ages
is pleasingly broad. The sample includes at least one respondent
from every year of age between eighteen and seventy-nine inclusive.
This means we have a series of testimonies from irregularly or nonpracticing Catholics born in each year from 1936 to 1997. As is clear
from figure 1, we received more testimonies from those of some
ages than others. In fact, almost three-fifths of all our respondents

---

several cases this was not so. This could be for several reasons. Most often it
was due to practicing Catholics wishing to share *their* story or to participate "on
behalf of" an inactive Catholic known to them. The team also received several
contributions, from individuals and groups, outside of the survey itself. While
we were interested to receive these, and they have indeed been helpful in
informing the research, we have nevertheless excluded them for the purposes of
our analysis. However, we *did* decide to include one special category of responses
that did not strictly meet our eligibility criteria. These were from participants
who fulfilled (a) to (c) but who had recently *returned* to regular Mass attendance.
Given the overarching purpose of the study, these respondents were felt to offer
an invaluable perspective.

(147 out of a total of 256) were between the ages of thirty-one and fifty-five. These characteristics of the sample, no doubt due to a combination of reasons,[3] are worth bearing in mind in all that follows. Over half of our respondents, for instance, were born after the Second Vatican Council (1962–65), and only one in seven would have been teenagers or older before the Council began.

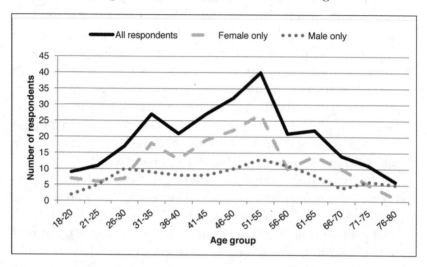

Figure 1. Age and Gender Breakdown of "MyStoryShared" Respondents

Of all the respondents, 63 percent currently live in the Diocese of Portsmouth and 16 percent used to live there. A further 21 percent neither live nor have lived there but have close family links to

---

3. Most obviously, it has long been established that women are more likely to respond to surveys than men, with recent research suggesting that the pattern also holds true for web surveys specifically (Smith 2008). Our use of an online survey may well have deterred some older respondents, while likely encouraging younger ones. More subtly, the very nature of a survey like this (i.e., explicitly asking people to *share their story*) would almost certainly recruit those who feel that they have a specific narrative to relate, rather than those who "just stopped going" for no reason or those who never really attended in the first place. Equally, one may suppose that inactive Catholics willing to make the (in some cases, extensive) time commitment to participate, to inform the Church why they have left, are disproportionately likely still to be "religiously interested" than those who are not. Given the higher levels of religiosity among women generally (see Trzebiatowska and Bruce 2012), this might explain the higher numbers of women in our sample.

the diocese. In terms of upbringing, 88 percent of participants said that they had been raised in a Catholic family. A further 3 percent, although they had been baptized Catholic, felt that theirs was not a "Catholic family" due to one parent, for example, being Catholic but not the other. The remaining 9 percent of our sample are what one might call "true converts." This is, incidentally, very close to the proportion of converts found in the Catholic population of England and Wales as a whole (i.e., 7.7 percent; Bullivant 2016a, 12). Among those who, when prompted, specified an age for their having become Catholic, the mean was twenty-six (SD = ten), with a range between fourteen and forty-seven.

Ninety-two percent of participants identified themselves as white; again, a figure very close to estimates in the Catholic population.[4] Two percent identified themselves as Asian, 1 percent as black, 4 percent as mixed origin, and 1 percent as other.

Finally, recall that this survey was targeted explicitly at Catholics "who no longer regularly practice their Faith." This admits of a wide degree of variation, especially bearing in mind the Church's formal prescription that "on Sundays and other holy days of obligation, the faithful are obliged to participate in the Mass" (Code of Canon Law, no. 1247). To a certain extent, we allowed respondents to decide for themselves how to interpret the criterion of "regular practice." However, we ultimately excluded as ineligible responses from weekly or fortnightly attenders (most of whom were responding "on behalf of" people known to them or who simply wished to offer their own views). These, however, were considered on a case-by-case basis, and a small number of exceptions were made. In most cases, these were people who had only recently returned to regular practice: an important source of information considering this book's interest in "Why They Might Return." In one case, a respondent, who for complicated personal reasons no longer attends Sunday Mass but does attend Mass on weekdays, was also judged eligible for inclusion. Given the Church's norm of Sunday

---

4. E.g., the 2012–14 data from the British Social Attitudes survey (excluding Scotland), put the proportion of whites among self-identifying Catholics at 88 percent. The 2014 data from the British Election Study, meanwhile, puts the proportion at 91 percent. (See Bullivant 2016a: 10, 18 no. 11.)

attendance, this was deemed to qualify as "irregular" (albeit, not infrequent) practice.

THE PURPOSE

The aim of this brief book is to provide a faithful summary of the main themes related by our participants, and to do so, as far as possible, in their own words. We hope that the many people who participated read it and feel adequately represented, even where we have not quoted them directly. However, we do not pretend to offer an exhaustive account of the responses received—running to tens of thousands of words—and the very many issues that they raised. It is intended rather as an illuminating, eye-opening, and ideally pastorally useful precis.[5] In all cases we have striven to present the complaints, disappointments, regrets, and hopes of our respondents at face value. In other words, we seek to offer an accurate record of the reasons nonpracticing Catholics *themselves* give for how this has come about. It is not our task, in this work, to attempt to answer or rebut them (although we do offer some pastoral recommendations in the conclusion). And it should be understood, naturally, that quotation does not imply endorsement.

Given the topic, there is admittedly much here that will, and indeed ought to, make for hard reading by many involved with the Catholic Church. This is especially so in chapter 1, where we probe the reasons why our respondents have left behind not just regular Mass-going, but, as for 27 percent of our respondents, even still regarding themselves as Catholic at all.[6] Nevertheless, there is also a good deal from which practicing Catholics might take heart. As the later chapters show, even among those distant from the Church for a long time, there is much that is still cherished and admired; for some (albeit a minority of) respondents, there is a genuine longing to return, which they hope, and in some cases fully expect, to fulfill.

---

5. In due course, we hope to publish further studies using the full dataset to explore specific issues more deeply.

6. A further 24 percent said that they regard themselves as Catholics "sometimes, but not always."

This book is divided into five chapters with each providing an overview of some of the main findings to emerge from our responses. These are grouped by subject. In our first two chapters, we address the question of *why* many Catholics no longer practice the Faith. Chapter 1 focuses on practical and experiential reasons; chapter 2 concentrates on intellectual, doctrinal, and moral ones. (Of course, and as will be abundantly clear, this neat division is to some degree artificial.) Chapter 3 explores what respondents miss about the Church. And chapter 4 gives their responses when asked what, if anything, the Church might do to entice them back. The fifth and concluding chapter offers some pastoral and theological reflections on the data and makes several concrete recommendations as to how Catholics, individually and collectively, might best respond to our findings.

Finally, we publicly thank all who took the time to respond to Bishop Philip's invitation to *share their story*.

1

WHY?—PRACTICAL AND EXPERIENTIAL REASONS

It is important to stress at the beginning that each person's story of how they have become distanced from the Church is unique, intimately bound up with his or her own individual biography. Without losing sight of this, it is possible to recognize recurring themes that are shared, albeit with considerable variation, across different narratives. Accordingly, this chapter identifies several broad, overarching patterns to different stories of distancing. For example, just under a third of respondents referred to a specific personal issue or incident as a main cause or trigger for ceasing to attend Mass regularly. These are wide-ranging: from altercations with clergy at every level to issues surrounding a respondent's marriage, and from parish politics to a family member's death. We include respondents' personal issues concerning marriage and sexuality, as well as the small number of respondents whose reasons for leaving relate to the sexual abuse crisis, through having suffered personally and/ or (more often) having been scandalized by the revelations.

We have grouped the assorted reasons cited into the following six broad "themes," most of which are then further divided into several subthemes:

1. Life Circumstances

2. Parochial Concerns

3. Spiritual and Liturgical Disillusionment

4. Attractions of Other Churches

5. Negative Experiences with Clergy

6. Sexual Abuse and the Church

Please note that our general themes are not mutually exclusive. An individual respondent's story, perhaps running to thousands of words and spanning several decades, might include several of these, at various times, and/or to different degrees. Relatively few of the stories we received fit neatly into one, and only one, of these abstracted "patterns." Informed readers will likely, and with ample justification, disagree with some of our specific placement decisions; that is the nature of this kind of research. Even where there is a clear, primary cause for a person no longer practicing regularly, this is often accompanied by other influencing factors. To give a simple example, a person who stops going to Mass because of family-related time pressures may often also disagree with Church teaching on certain points and find the liturgical style at their local parish too informal. In this case, although the time pressure is the immediate and primary cause, the other two factors are hardly irrelevant: perhaps if one or both were not present, there would remain sufficient motivation to find a more convenient Mass time or prioritize Sunday obligations over other family activities.

It is partly for this reason that, in contrast with some other studies, we have made no attempt to divide our respondents into specific social or psychological "types" (cf. Hoge et al. 1981; Streib et al. 2009). We also make sparing use of percentages. While it is sometimes useful to state, for example, that "about a third of our respondents cited x as a factor in their own distancing from the Church" (since this gives a general impression of its prevalence), we avoid making claims of the kind "14.7 percent of inactive Catholics are so because of y." Such *apparent* precision is nothing but misleading, given both the nature of our sample and the difficulties of weighing the relative effects of different factors (not all of which, of course, may be apparent to the respondents themselves).

LIFE CIRCUMSTANCES

For some respondents, their practice or nonpractice was highly contingent upon external pressures. These include whether they are living at home with parents and family, whether there is a convenient Mass time, how busy life is, or whether illness or other family circumstances hinder their attendance. In many cases, the effects of these are not sudden but rather accumulate over time. As one of our respondents stated, "It's the insignificant things that tend to build up and push people away" (female, 42).

Over half of our respondents agreed or strongly agreed that they "gradually lost interest in going to Mass." We might say that these reasons concern, first and foremost, a person's lived experience, both of everyday life and of the Church's significance. Other factors are not normally irrelevant here. However, they tend not to be so strong as either to be the main push away from, or a counteracting pull toward, continuing attendance.

Growing up and Empty Nests

As is evident from previous studies, the mid to late teens often mark a major watershed in religious practice, as in much else (e.g., Hoge et al. 1981, 97–105). Two moments emerge as particularly significant, whether as a sudden and deliberate dropping-off point or as marking the beginning of a more gradual and unplanned "drift." The first of these is the time when family Mass attendance is no longer insisted upon, that is, when parents leave the decision of whether to go or not up to their children.

> I attended Mass every Sunday when I was growing up and living with my parents. Once I moved out of the family home, I stopped attending. My lifestyle and daily routine had changed and attending Mass fell down my priority list until it seemed to filter out completely. This was not a conscious decision but a slowly realized side effect of a lifestyle change. (female, 25)
>
> Up until my mid-teens, I attended Mass regularly. I disliked attending Church because I felt that I could communicate with God by myself, somewhere quiet without distractions. (female, 53)
>
> Once I was no longer "required" to attend Mass at the request of my parents—at age 18—I stopped going. I had stopped believing by age 14. (male, 32)

The second such moment comes when young adults leave the family home, most usually to attend university:

> When I lived at home with my parents, I attended Mass on a regular basis. When I left home to go to university, that stopped. (male, 35)
>
> In leaving home, I did not feel the need to go to church anymore, and that feeling has never really changed. (male, 47)

Often this change was not an intentional decision:

> Until I left home to go to university, I went to Mass with my family every Sunday. I stopped going as soon as I didn't have my mum and dad watching over me. It wasn't down to a lack of faith, just pure laziness. (male, 35)

While many respondents were content enough with Mass-going as part of a family habit or routine, others resented regular attendance as something imposed, explicitly or implicitly, against their will:

> I didn't have a choice to go to Mass growing up. When I had the choice, I decided "No." (male, 39)
>
> As a child there was no choice; you just followed your parents and were never asked if this was something that you wanted to do. (female, 21)
>
> We would go to Mass every Sunday but also every day as soon as the school holidays began. Maybe being forced into this amount

of worship made it into a chore—there was no joy in it at all and I resented going as I got older. (female, 30)

Religion was forced down my throat by my father, a devout Catholic. (female, 40)

I made that decision at 13, but I didn't want to abandon my mum [the only other Catholic in a religiously mixed family], as she seemed very alone in our family. She was also quite depressed and angry, I feared how she would react if I told her I wasn't going to church any more. So, I carried on going to church, even though I'd decided I wanted to stop, until I was 18 years old. (female, 42)

Some suggest either that they had stopped believing years before their practice ended or that their spiritual experience was at odds with what they thought was expected. They reflect on the pressures to practice that had accompanied those years:

I felt that my religion was forced upon me by my family and am now much happier given the option of choice when it comes to Church. (female, 18)

Looking back, I regret making my Confirmation and should have had the courage to be honest with my family at the time. (male, 24)

Religion had an air of quite excruciating embarrassment about it and was never discussed at home. When I objected to going to church in my teens, my views were not listened to nor respected. Looking back now, I think I was poorly catechized, despite regular catechism lessons. Belief was assumed. No one ever took me through arguments for the existence of God....When I went to university, I started off by regular Mass attendance but then it dawned on me that I was now free to do as I wished and gradually tailed off. (female, 51)

As a child in the 1950s, I had no choice and was brought up to accept parental decisions....I felt I became a more thoughtful and committed Christian when I joined the Christian Union at secondary school. The people were both intelligent and kind, and we were encouraged to think as well as study the Bible, which we never did in Church....Later at university, I very occasionally went to Mass with friends but didn't get anything out of it. I went to Mass with my mum when visiting home but just felt guilty because it was so boring. Not going would upset her but going made me feel hypocritical. (female, 63)

In most cases, practicing or believing as a Catholic was not supplanted with any other significant religious commitment. Take, for example, this detailed account of gradual distancing:

I used to go to Mass regularly until I was 18 or 19 years old, never missing a Sunday or holy day of obligation. I believed sincerely and devotedly in God as the source of love, humanity, and goodness. I continued to go to church even as my faith wavered, praying for hope and understanding. I continue to believe in the ideals that I was brought up with, such as loving my neighbor as much (or more) than myself. But gradually, I found that Sunday Mass had less to teach me, no answers to give me, and no one I knew (and I knew many kind, sweet Catholics) could give me any answers. No one faith seemed better than any other, and the warm comfort and familiarity of Catholicism wasn't enough to sustain my desire to go to church. I don't go to church (except for baptisms, funerals, weddings) and I live my life happily, but I still haven't found the answers I was looking for all those years ago. (female, 54)

However, for a small number of respondents, growing disillusionment with the Church coincided with attraction toward a different denomination or, less often, religion. (See "Attraction of Other

Churches" below for other accounts from those not in this specific age/life-stage group.)

> [At university] I met diverse groups of people, with different beliefs, practices and personal experiences. I started to feel the Masses I attended bland and listless. There wasn't a sense of transformation in people due to their faith. There wasn't the support or connection I wanted. I started going to a Church of England parish church, which was very welcoming, and they had a really good service. (male, 34)
>
> I stopped, or at least went less, until I was about 19. I then joined a Christian group at university and made friends there. Many of them were connected to a local church offering Bible study, cell groups and social events. I didn't see any reason to go back to attending the Catholic Church once I settled in here....I got baptized in this group (my Catholic baptism wasn't sufficient) and I saw no reason to identify as a Catholic. I don't see most Catholics as informed or living out the Gospel, attending Mass always seemed more a habit and not an inner work of the Spirit. (male, 27)
>
> I drifted away after school and got occupied with other things. When I was 19, I converted to Islam after doing research and making a few friends. (female, 23)

A surprising corollary follows from this wide trend of people who stop practicing in young adulthood. There is an additional, though more marginal, thread of parents who stopped attending once *their children* no longer attended.

> [Having had a period of non-practice as a young adult], I started to go regularly again once I had children because I wanted to raise them as Catholics. They went to children's liturgy, which I believe

they enjoyed. Once they started at their Catholic secondary school, I gave them the option of attending Mass, which they declined. I stopped going again because the homily was dull, never relevant, and read from a piece of paper with no substance to it. (female, 47)

My daughter made her Confirmation then not long after said that there were so many things she didn't agree with that she couldn't continue to go to Mass. We talked a lot about the Catholic Church, and I found that there were so many things I didn't agree with either that it would have been hypocritical to continue going to church....Gradually we both stopped going. (female, 54)

Drifting Away

Overlapping with those in the above category are those relating how, over time, they simply "drifted away" from the Church. In many cases, there was no conscious decision to leave—it "just happened."

My departure from the Church was a slow one and took place over several years. It started when I became a single parent in my early 30s when my wife left me. While I continued attending Mass and remained very active in parish affairs, I felt increasingly isolated and got the sense that my situation couldn't be discussed. I began to miss the occasional Sunday Mass and then stopped going altogether at the weekend. I carried on going during the week in the city where I work, and then I stopped. And then I stopped going to Mass, just calling into church to pray. This stopped completely about five years ago. (male, 53)

When I joined the navy aged 16, I still attended Mass but over the years, the more and more time I spent at sea with no opportunity for Mass, the less and less frequently I attended when I had the chance. I lost the habit. (male, 64)

8

In others, a prolonged period of drifting away led ultimately to the recognition that Mass no longer played a significant role in the person's life. This realization, often coupled with one or more other reasons for dissatisfaction, then triggered a more definite resolution. One man who had become a Catholic at the age of twenty-three said,

> Mass was a ritual that was just done without any thought. The more I examined my life and my purpose and spirituality, the more I realized that Mass was not part of my life. (male, 46)

Lives, Busy and Difficult

While most respondents disagreed that their work and personal schedules prevented them from attending Mass, many did nevertheless cite the busyness of lives as an inhibiting factor:

> I can't find the time. Job, motherhood, and housework take up most of my time. (female, 35)
>
> When my daughter was first born, I attended Sunday Mass most weeks with my husband....We wanted to make churchgoing part of our lives. Our children attended a Catholic school; we felt part of the Catholic community. However, our lives have become very busy and complex, and Sunday mornings have been taken up with other family activities. (female, 45)
>
> Children growing up and playing sports on a Sunday morning makes it difficult to attend. On Saturday and Sunday evenings, we have family time by sitting down and sharing a meal—so I am reluctant to break this routine. We try to go to Mass at 9 a.m. as often as possible so we can get to football/rugby matches afterwards. (female, 45)

I work long hours, so I get the weekends only to focus purely on family but also try and fit in all chores and everything that doesn't take place during the week. Life is currently so busy I don't get five minutes, let alone an hour to attend Mass. (female, 38)

Now I work, have a family, and on the weekend, I want to sleep for as long as I can because on Monday the run will start again. (female, 33)

Relatedly, some respondents found that local Mass times were not sufficiently convenient:

Now elderly, we are not always well enough to travel a distance to Mass. Mass times were changed and are now too early. The later family Masses are too long. Nobody has visited us from the parish to find out how we are or why we are seldom at Mass. (female, 75)

I attended Mass regularly when I was young. Then I started work and moved away from home. Really poor excuse, but the times of Mass do not suit me. (male, 49)

Interestingly, the latter respondent's note of awkwardness about offering this kind of reason was one shared with others:

Life's also busy and perhaps an excuse but there's always something pressing at the weekends, e.g., DIY, exercise, catching up with friends, family and general life. (male, 36)

I have a busy life and children and just got out of the habit of going to Mass, but thinking about it, I don't know why I don't go now. I need to find someone to go with as I will feel awkward after so long. It seems like a feeble excuse. (female, 65)

Rather different are those who, due to difficult personal circumstances, find going to Mass very hard, in practical terms or emotionally. These respondents stand out in the sample—though they are by no means the only ones—in typically expressing significant regret or sorrow in their lack of attendance:

After my mum's funeral, I found it too emotional going to Mass. Hymns bring tears to my eyes. (female, 30)

I attended Mass every Sunday until the last eight years, after I moved. I intended to keep going to Mass, but things happened in my life which pushed me away from my faith. It's got to a stage now when I keep saying I will go to church this Sunday, but for some reason I find an excuse not to go. (male, 45)

Since my mother became housebound and I started caring daily for her and my father, I found it difficult to find the time or was too exhausted or was trying to look after my own family. Although I still prayed daily and would watch EWTN for Mass, I still felt very guilty for not attending Mass. (female, 48)

I am currently attending about once every six weeks. [Among several other reasons] is tiredness due to pressure of work and looking after my 93-year-old mother. Sunday is my one day off. (female, 62)

Finally, a small group of people said it was their difficulties in going to confession (that is, as a necessary precursor to receiving holy communion) that were their main obstacles to returning to Mass. The specific reasons given here were mixed, including practical, doctrinal, and personal ones:

My biggest barrier to attending Church is the doctrine around not being able to receive Communion if one has missed a week, without having to go to Confession first! I hate that, if I go to Mass with my parents, I'm made to feel guilty by the Church if I do "break the rules" and receive Communion, but by not receiving, I disappoint my family because it's then obvious that I choose not to observe my faith in the same way they do. (female, 42)

As a teenager I felt too embarrassed to confess my sins, so I drifted away. (female, 33)

For the last few years, I have attended Mass intermittently because sometimes I have missed it for trivial reasons. Consequently, I need to attend Confession and the timings for that do not suit me.... Because I have to attend Confession in order to receive Holy Communion, I keep missing Mass when actually I would like to go. (female, 45)

PAROCHIAL CONCERNS

The many issues grouped under this broad heading can be summarized by saying that all, in some way, involve a form of disconnection between the parishioner and parish community. This disconnection comes in many forms: unwelcoming atmospheres, lack of experience of community, parishioners who feel neglected or ignored when undergoing hardships, feelings of being unappreciated or taken for granted.

True, a majority did not cite community issues as a reason for leaving the Church, and, as we will see in the next chapter, community is one of the things that is most missed. Nevertheless, roughly two-fifths of respondents either agreed or strongly agreed with the following statement: "I am uncomfortable with the feeling of community in my parish." Many referred to specific, personal complaints; in several cases, more or less similar accounts appeared in multiple responses. Meanwhile, some wrote in more general terms about either a lack of community or with a negative appraisal of what community there was. One respondent spoke of there being "[nothing serious] but relentless little disappointments and failures that didn't help at the time" (female, 55). Or, in the poignant question of another: "Maybe my expectations of a church community were too high?" (female, 51).

Unfriendliness and Cliquishness

Lack of welcome and/or a culture of cliquishness were frequent themes in many responses:

It's not just one person; it is the general attitude. I felt unwelcome. (male, 28)

I used to attend Mass every week and was very active in the parish. I moved to another diocese and started to attend Mass, but priests and parishioners were not very welcoming. Not a lot going on in the parish. (male, 55)

I became disillusioned with the parish priest and the infrastructure of both the parish and the diocesan organization....My brief association with the Catenians[1] (an association of Catholic laymen) was another nail in the coffin. (male, 51)

Despite trying to get involved at every level (school, Mass, activities like helping with teas), I never felt that my face "fitted"....No one was very friendly, and it felt very cliquey. (female, 66)

There are cliques in every parish who control the parish. (female, 68)

In certain cases, it seems, these kinds of group cultures were experienced as being actively hostile.

---

1. The Catenians are an association of Catholic laymen who are committed to their Faith, their families, to those in need, and to each other. Their primary purpose is to establish a network of friends, which enhances their family life, strengthens their Faith, and sustains them in challenging times. See https://www.thecatenians.com.

Too many nasty, judgmental people like to put themselves close to the center of parishes. (female, 45)

In my church, there was a lot of arguments and hostile behavior between some members of the congregation and the priest. (female, 21)

Character assassination, backbiting and general "judginess" was commonplace, and it was vile. (female, 45)

Lack of Contact or Concern

For several respondents, lack of contact from their parish when they had (for several reasons) been absent for a time made them think that nobody either noticed or cared if they were there or not.

I attended Mass every Sunday until the tsunami in 2004. The tsunami, though I was not personally affected, made me question some core beliefs: that a deity can be all powerful, all knowing and all loving at the same time....I had been told that church meant the people, not the building, and that the richness in the church was in the community. It's entirely possible that I'm an unapproachable person. Yet not one member of the congregation ever called, came over, or bothered to ask me why I had suddenly stopped coming. (male, 42)

I was very active in my local church, in a listening group, as a catechist, a cleaner, and any other thing that I was asked to do. About two years ago, I had a rather bad year with being ill, [other family issues], and the death of my brother. Though the church did not know all my troubles, they knew about my brother, but no one from the parish inquired after me. I stopped attending Mass regularly, and again no one, not even my parish priest, inquired after me. (female, 46)

Having missed several weeks, I wrote to the priest and sent him a check for the Sundays I had missed to keep my weekly donations up to date. I said my lack of appearance at Mass was due to family difficulties. No acknowledgement of my letter, and there was no attempt to find out if I needed any help. (female, 62)

As our testimonies indicate, parishioners feel this (perceived) lack of concern and support even more when dealing with serious personal difficulties, including ill health and marital crises.

Five years ago, I became unwell and was unable to attend every week. Eventually, attending Mass became both physically and emotionally challenging....The person who brought me Holy Communion had a breakdown and stopped coming. That was eighteen months ago. I have had Communion brought to me three times since. I don't like to ask for more, as I know the parish volunteers are stretched, so I am beginning to feel disconnected from my parish....Sometimes, I feel that I put so much into helping others in the parish when I was able, but now I only have occasional contact from maybe three or four members of the parish. (female, 50)

I used to attend Mass daily. Through ill health and bereavement, I became alienated from a community who offered no support when requested. When I lay critically ill in hospital, the chaplain didn't respond to a request for a visit. As somebody who worked for Catholic chaplaincies around the country, I struggled with this. (male, 51)

When my marriage broke up, everyone knew. One week we were sitting together as a family; the next, we were sitting apart. We were in pain and it seemed like everyone just looked away. It is hard to ask for help, but the church community I thought we were part of could have helped. (male, 60)

Slightly differently, a few respondents wrote that the lack of recognition of their contributions to the parish led them to drift away:

> We were made very welcome when we joined the Catholic Church
> (when I was 43). My husband became a special minister, and I
> organized the rota, programs, and led the children's liturgy for
> several years. Over that time, there were several different priests
> who took little or no interest in what was happening in the chil-
> dren's liturgy. When I "retired" from my liturgical responsibilities,
> I was surprised and disappointed not to have even an acknowl-
> edgement of my work with and for the children. (female, 66)

> Despite having regularly attended the church, organized a fund-
> raiser charity sale, and donated through the envelope system over
> a period of 25 years, no one has ever introduced themselves to me
> or in any way invited me to take part in the church activities.
> (female, 62)

Children and Families

Inadequate provision for or acceptance of children at Mass
was a recurrent theme that was very often considered a "deal
breaker." In other words, parents—and, judging from our sample,
mothers in particular[2]—do not want to go somewhere where they
feel that their children are unwanted.

> Unfortunately, despite offering to organize a group for younger
> children, the church said no. My little one is four years old, so
> sitting through a service quietly is not easy or relaxing. The books

---

2. Without wishing to downplay the importance of this issue, it is perhaps
worth noting that its prevalence in our study is perhaps related to the specific
demographics of our sample (i.e., disproportionate numbers of women—who
were far more likely than men to cite this type of issue—and those aged in their
thirties and forties).

supplied for the use of little children are broken. Children learn through play. So, I joined an Anglican church that has a Sunday school for all ages who make and learn things throughout the year, not just term time. (female, 42)

We moved, and our new parish had no activities for children. I offered to start a brownie pack but was turned down because "the hall had a new wooden floor, and we cannot have children running around and ruining it!" I enrolled my children into another church's pack. They loved the church and asked to go to Sunday school. We all benefited from many happy years in that parish, but I always wished the Catholic Church could have been as welcoming. (female, 69)

I have an inquisitive young girl with whom I have loved sharing the joy of the Church, but she learns far more from me when I take her into an empty church and can talk (quietly) about the statues, the different things on the sanctuary, the candles, why they are there, what it means, etcetera, than she will ever do at Mass where she cannot see or hear what is happening but only the person's back in front of her, where the liturgy is spoken in a language that means nothing to her, and in which she as a person is totally ignored....So, why should I take her, what is the point? I take the children on my own as my husband isn't a Catholic....It is Christmas Eve tomorrow, and for the first time ever, I am considering taking my children to an Anglican church instead of a Catholic one, since they have a "crib service." (female, 33)

I have been horrified at how unwelcoming our church has been to young children and mums. When my children were babies, the lack of friendliness of my parish's "toddler group" and the way in which our priest has made it clear that children should be silent at Mass has really annoyed me—it's so far from what the church should be. (female, 37)

Attempted Returns

Striking a somewhat different note, some respondents spoke of their attempts to return to Mass over the years, with disappointing results.

> When I left home and moved away, I attended Mass occasionally for a while. I then moved to a different parish when I got married and attended Mass there at Easter. The priest who said Mass said in his homily that if you are a "Christmas and Easter Catholic," you have no place in the church. At the time, I was wanting to come back to my faith, but this one comment made me feel I wasn't worthy. (female, 50)
>
> I stopped attending Mass because I no longer felt any connection with the body of the church. In fact, although I have in the last few months started to attend Mass after being away for more than 35 years, I still feel that disconnection. (female, 53)

For another person who tried a few times to reconnect, it was her online experience that was off-putting:

> The last time I shied away was in a conversation on a Catholic Facebook page. It was in a discussion about gender roles. I found the comments of some of the other respondents so polemical that I didn't want to be in the conversation any more. My heart closed again. (female, 42)

SPIRITUAL AND LITURGICAL DISILLUSIONMENT

Three-fifths of respondents either agreed or strongly agreed that "my spiritual needs were not being met." For Catholics, not surprisingly, "spiritual needs" (or "wants") are intimately connected with the liturgy. Given the centrality of liturgy as "the summit toward which the activity of the Church is directed; at the same time it is the font from which all her power flows" (*Sacrosanctum Concilium* 10), it follows that liturgical disillusionment can have an overarching effect on the totality of a person's life as a Christian. Dislike of a form or style of liturgical worship can often hinder feelings of having gained any spiritual "benefit" from being there. In other words, someone for whom Mass has "become an intensely boring chore that seemed to ruin the last morning of the weekend" (male, 26) is unlikely to carry a powerful sense of Catholic commitment and identity into the rest of their week—or at least is unlikely to manage to do so for long. As another stated, "I need to go to church to be filled up and not drained" (male, 54).

At the more extreme end, two respondents felt, for very different reasons, that they *oughtn't* to attend Mass to fulfill their spiritual needs:

I gladly stopped as a teenager when not made to attend Mass. But it never went away and, when my children were teenagers, I went back, and it was a relief. Along the way, I was niggled with doubts. This went on for years and, one day in his sermon, the priest said something about people going to Mass to fulfil their spiritual needs. That I thought was me, I didn't want to be a hypocrite and soon after stopped going. (female, 67)

Masses have become increasingly less Catholic—they don't value the traditions and culture of Catholicism and seem confused. This makes me feel sad and wonder where our traditions have gone and why priests don't want to pass the true Faith on to the next generation. I find I am more able to stay true to my faith when I am away from church than when I attend and find my traditional faith at odds with what is being taught and practiced now. (female, 33)

Those familiar with church life will probably not be surprised at the very wide, and often mutually exclusive, range of criticisms made in this area. Clearly, there is no one Mass that can satisfy everyone.

Boredom, Irrelevance, Backwardness

For a sizable number, the liturgy was felt to be too "dull" or irrelevant to their actual lives:

I think the Catholic service, or at least the ones I attended, were sometimes somber and joyless. And if we are coming together to worship, surely it should be the opposite. (female, 30)

Mass is dull, lifeless and completely "unrelatable." The homily at my local church is a lecture for very intelligent and indulged Catholics on theory and other things. It goes way over my head and is not of interest. I gained nothing from it. (male, 18)

I was doing my duty for my children but did not particularly feel enlightened after Mass. I felt disconnected because the readings are what they are, but there isn't very often connection to the world around us. Hence, boredom set in. (female, 52)

Mass was sometimes boring, with dreary, cranky hymns—none of the wonderful ones we learnt at school (e.g., "The Lord Is My Shepherd" or other uplifting ones). (female, 53)

I don't go anymore because it is hard to relate to, and not up-to-date; it can be boring for young people like me. (female, 20)

We have tried to continue attending Mass regularly, but it is no longer a pleasant and friendly experience. Even the liturgy is tedious and dreary. (male, 62)

One respondent commented specifically on the noncharismatic nature of parish liturgy. (Similar themes are raised by those respondents who have more satisfactory ecclesial homes outside the Catholic Church; see "Attractions of Other Churches" below.)

> I became a Catholic charismatic and enjoyed the freedom that the Spirit gave me, however, my increased love for God was not nurtured by the priest or other members of the church....My son, too, was very Spirit-filled but felt stifled by the church we went to. We found another Catholic church to attend and did so for some time, but again, it was not open to the Holy Spirit. (female, 56)

For many, there is a general perception that the Church is presently moving in the wrong direction, that is, "backward," regarding the liturgy. Several commented on recent changes within their own parishes, often linked with the arrival of new (and younger) clergy, which were thought to be retrograde.

> The recent changes in the Church—moving back to more traditional outlooks and practices—have felt very alienating. I am a child of Vatican II. I neither really know nor relish the "old ways," and am no longer a "young person." Surely, I am very much the mainstream at the age of 52? (female, 52)
>
> To fit in with the parish, you need to be over 65 and like traditional pre-Vatican II-style liturgies with lengthy Benedictions and nineteenth-century hymns. (male, 58)
>
> What has changed? The fear of priests who have, in my local area, gone back to "childhood," it seems, and who mention such things as the more attendance at Mass equals a better chance to get into heaven, as if some loyalty card exists! I thought such nonsense had disappeared after Vatican II....Also, this obsession with the

> past, with Latin, with absolutism, with the perfect liturgy, with a male-dominated Church, with priests telling married couples what is right and what is wrong. It's so wrong and dysfunctional. My children have long left, angry, yet continue to have deep faith and an understanding of the love of God. They cannot understand why those who lead in the Church are so joyless! We are going backwards! (male, 53)

With a number of these commenters, the "new translation" of the Mass introduced across England and Wales in Advent 2010 was singled out as exemplifying this overall trend.

> The new Mass language is awful, patriarchal, and presents an image of God I cannot accept! We need to start again with a more inclusive language and image of God as a loving and merciful Father! (male, 65)
>
> There is poor liturgy in many parishes and the new translation of the missal is very clumsy. The Church should use language that people without theological qualifications can understand. (male, 56)
>
> The Mass changed back from the modern Mass of Vatican II, and I felt this was a backward step. (female, 27)
>
> I left the Church very soon after the appalling mangling of the language of the Mass began. I was already very unhappy at the way the Church was moving, back to the 1950s and rolling back the opening up of Vatican II....The language and outward appearance of the Church lurched back into the nineteenth century while the rest of the world embraced the twenty-first century, for me the imposition of the new translation was the final straw. (female, 53)
>
> The changes in language used in the Mass over the last few years have made the ceremony less accessible, more "high," and less in touch with the congregation. (male, 47)

Lack of Reverence and Tradition

For a considerable number of respondents, however, it was a lack of reverence or respect—indeed, for some, of what they perceived to be being "properly Catholic"—that was the overriding concern.

As a child, going to church involved attending the children's liturgy until I was confirmed. This probably slowly destroyed my faith....It was all very banal. All but one of my Catholic friends has left the Church....There is no order; people are constantly talking before, during, and after; people wear revealing clothes. I just don't see it as worshipping God. To me it is just a feminized worshipping of mankind. (male, 24)

I have had issues with the noise level and lack of respect in our Masses....There is now a high noise level with phones going off and children running around, people talking about football and the new shoes that they have bought, etcetera. Special dates, such as Easter and Christmas, can be like a circus. I have walked out before Communion because it has been so noisy. I leave Mass feeling very unchristian and quite stressed. (female, 46)

I attended daily Mass for years but gradually found that discipline declined in Church matters. The reverence and respect for the Mass has declined over the past twenty years. Now to hope to be able to prepare for Mass is impossible because the atmosphere is that of a theatre with people wandering around chatting, and children with picnics! I appreciate that the Church has "moved on," but it is not the Church that I loved so much. (female, 73)

As I get older, I am losing the will to put up with what seems to me a very spiritually empty liturgy....Mass is more like a primary school assembly; everyone is very busy with different tasks, but it becomes impossible to connect with God. (female, 61)

I stopped going [because] I felt alienated during services as they had become all-singing, all-dancing productions...more like a show than prayer....I wanted a simple, humble, quiet service. As I don't drive, no other church was available to me. (female, 50)

I will not receive Communion from [Extraordinary Ministers of Holy Communion] unless in a cathedral or other situations where they are supposed to be used because there are not enough priests or deacons. I dislike the way the [Sign of Peace] is presently conducted; and its position during the Mass. (female, 70)

As we will observe in the second chapter, these kinds of liturgical criticisms often allied with criticisms of much broader trends in the Catholic Church over the past several decades. Here we might note, considering the complaints in the above subsection about the Church harking back to pre–Vatican II times, that here, too, unflattering parallels are also often drawn to certain, albeit more recent, time periods.

The churches are ugly, the music is stuck in the 1970s...hippy Masses straight out of 1972. (male, 24)

My family found the various changes to the Mass and various practices over the past fifty years unsettling. Many family members have left since the 70s. Some clergy and religious haven't helped because they used changes and uncertainty to push on with their own ideas. I'm not against change, but I always felt there was some dishonesty or self-delusion going on when people acted like the changes were a success. My family associate decline and pain with those changes and this hasn't been addressed by the Church. It's like the Church can never admit any mistakes. (female, 42)

> In the 1980s, the Church went barking mad. In my parish, the church I attended then was basically vandalized: The Stations of the Cross were painted over and replaced with modern abstracts; the altar and altar rails removed and replaced by a table; the crucifix was removed from above the altar; a new parish priest encouraged weird behavior during Mass, people were dashing about giving the [Sign of Peace] and waving their arms....It wasn't the Church I had joined. (female, 70)

Interestingly, in this connection, slightly over 10 percent of our sample either agreed or strongly agreed with the following statement: "I prefer the Latin Mass but there is none in my area."

ATTRACTIONS OF OTHER CHURCHES

In other countries, most notably the United States, there is a significant trend of cradle Catholics "switching" to other Christian denominations (Pew Research Center 2009; Center for Applied Research in the Apostolate 2008). This trend is far less evidenced in Britain, where Catholics, as in most other mainstream denominations, do not typically join—or desire to join—other churches, having become disillusioned with their own (e.g., Bullivant 2016b).

In our sample, however, this phenomenon was notably more common than in the population at large: around one in five of our respondents agreed or strongly agreed with the following statement: "I found a religion/denomination that I like more."[3] According to one respondent, who now identifies as an "Evangelical/ New Frontiers" Christian,

---

3. As noted in the footnotes to the previous chapter, it is reasonable to assume that the methodology adopted for this study would have yielded a more religiously interested sample than is typical of inactive Catholics as a whole. In other words, one might expect that eligible people who both heard that the Bishop of Portsmouth wanted them to "share their story," and who then actually took the time to do so, would include a disproportionate number of people still involved with and/or interested with religion.

> We searched around and eventually joined a church with good children's work, loads of teenagers, and young adults all involved with church life. There were midweek Bible study/prayer groups and all sorts of other things going on. The move was probably the best thing we have ever done. (female, 44)

For two more respondents, both of whom now describe themselves simply as "Christian":

> I decided that I wanted to explore my faith and the most accessible route was through an Alpha course at a non-Catholic church.... Being raised as a Catholic, I still feel a loyalty to the Church but, when compared to my experience at my new church, I feel less connected to God. (male, 31)
>
> My husband is a committed Methodist and is training to be a lay preacher. I have chosen to support him in the vocation and therefore regularly attend services which he is taking around his circuit of churches. We are both part of the charismatic renewal and are currently attending a church plant from HTB [Holy Trinity Brompton] in London together, as they have a service with a time that suits us on a Sunday evening. It is a church where we can really see God's Holy Spirit moving, and we want to be part of this. (female, 53)

Others have found a spiritual home in the Church of England:

> As a family we now attend a Church of England church every week. Unlike the Catholic service, which were very difficult to get my children to attend, the Church of England services are very inspirational, and my children really like attending. (male, 41)

One day, I went by chance to a local Anglican church where the welcome was overwhelming, and the teachings of the Bible are taught and lived out daily in our parish. (female, 66)

I used to attend our local Catholic church every week, but I haven't attended since I was 24. I didn't feel that I needed to go to church weekly. Then, when I got married to my Anglican wife, I was perfectly happy to attend the Anglican church that was in our village as opposed to the Catholic one which was a little further away. (male, 35)

Although we tried to attend Mass once a month, it was a chore and not a pleasure. My children got involved in "Messy Church" through the Church of England, and after attending this for a while we were invited to a service. My children loved "Messy Church" and really liked the service. We did not have to keep them quiet or send them out to be talked at and then color in at the children's liturgy....We were welcomed and involved in the service. We also felt a real sense of community and faith, in a way that the Catholic Church did not....My wife, and now my son, have become involved in running the local "Messy Church," and my wife and I have attended an Alpha course which has brought us to a new understanding and level of faith. I am certain that if we had carried on with the Catholic Mass this would not have happened. (male, 41)

NEGATIVE EXPERIENCES WITH CLERGY

In a previous section, we summarized respondents' issues, both general and specific, with various aspects of parish community life. Here, we focus on negative experiences with the members of the clergy. Such experiences, however, were by no means universal. In fact, fewer than one in three respondents either agreed or strongly agreed that the unfriendliness of a priest was a factor in their ceasing to attend Mass. Indeed, several respondents made a point of stressing that the opposite was the case. Take, for example, this testimony from a young man who drifted away from regular church attendance in his late teens:

I have never had an unpleasant experience with anyone at church. I served as an altar boy, and really looked up to and admired the parish priest. Everyone involved with the church was always open and friendly to me. (male, 29)

Nevertheless, given the significance of the clergy within the Catholic tradition when issues did occur, these were taken particularly to heart by respondents. A single traumatic incident, even if it happened many decades ago, could exert a powerful influence over a person's overall perception of, and feelings toward, the Church. These problems can take many forms, and here we seek to offer a representative sample. (The next section of this chapter will provide other examples, where clashes with clergy occur within the broader context of doctrinal issues.)

In most of these cases, respondents report a negative impression of a priest or priests based upon personal observation:

About a year ago, I was in the local pub, sat near a priest, and was listening to him bitch about a fellow priest—not for me. (female, 53)

We got a new priest in our parish, and I felt the Church was no longer as important as he felt he was. (female, 50)

At monthly First Communion Mass, the church is full of families with children preparing for their First Communion. Our priest uses this opportunity to tell people off and berate people for not coming more often and to ask for money, including handing out direct debit forms during Mass....This behavior made me feel embarrassed to be part of the parish and stopped me coming to church. (female, 32)

> The priests just go through the motions of saying Mass as if it is an intrusion to their time, no openness, no inclusion. If I contributed at Mass to the same level as the recently appointed priests, then there would be no responses and no singing. (male, 54)

Allied to these kinds of criticisms are those making a general comment on "priests as a whole," or at least the specific culture that they inhabit: "clericalism and institutionalism from the Vatican downwards" (male, 76).[4] In some cases, this is simply an unelaborated claim of clericalism.

However, a small number of participants reported specific episodes of a more personally traumatic nature:

> At 15 years of age, pregnant and ashamed, I went into the confessional to ask for absolution....In a rage, Father [X] dragged me out of the confessional into the vestry and told me that I had broken every commandment, broken my mother's heart, and was so sinful that he demanded that I leave the church immediately. Sadly, I never returned. (female, 71)

> Recently, I went to Confession to say that I had felt totally abandoned by the Church and God. I felt suicidal. I do not know if the priest heard me, but I left having been absolved in floods of tears. Later that day my husband took me to the hospital for help. (female, 42)

A few respondents referred specifically to an incident related to a family member's funeral:

---

4. Interestingly, this respondent elaborates: "Non-attendance in my own parish is the only way I can protest against the clericalism of the Church. It is not a reaction to our present parish priest or previous ones, or to fellow parishioners, since our parish, on the whole, is a good one and has been well served."

At one point when organizing my father's funeral, we were told that there was no one available to do the funeral and it wasn't his, i.e., the current priest's responsibility. My father had helped build our church, raise hundreds of thousands of pounds to fund it, and even prior to his death not one local priest would come and give him his last rites as it wasn't their job! (female, 49)

The priest refused to do the eulogy at my mother's funeral and said that he didn't like non-church music at a funeral. I had wanted a song by Jim Reeves played as the coffin was being carried from the church. I was horrified by his callous attitude and manner....At times like this, you want empathy and consideration, and I got neither. I have not stepped foot inside my church since the day of my mum's funeral and will not again until this priest is moved elsewhere. (female, 56)

Finally, some respondents focused their criticisms not on a specific parish priest, but rather more generally on the members of a religious order or congregation.

As a young Catholic I went to a convent primary school. I fully believed in what I was taught. But, as I grew up—in a broken home, post-war—and achieved some independence of thought, and became free of the "hellfire and brimstone" teachings of the religious congregation, I slowly realized how biased they were. Their arrogance that only the Catholics were "right" about religion, their intolerance of such things as divorce, abortion, birth control, etcetera, and the financial greed of the Catholic Church in general, were so high-handed and bigoted that clearly there was no true humanity in any of their works. (male, 77)

Another factor that deeply affected me, having known the order of priests in my parish personally, was the rich life they led and the way they treated parishioners by always giving the impression they were poor. They lived a rich life wanting for nothing when some parishioners lived in deep poverty. (female, 73)

SEXUAL ABUSE AND THE CHURCH

Closely related to the previous subheading, but evidently deserving of a separate section, is the "abuse scandal"—or rather, series of scandals—engulfing the Catholic Church, here and abroad, over the past several decades, although the instances of physical and sexual abuse, and subsequent cover-ups, often go much further back. Around half of all respondents either agreed or strongly agreed that the scandals in the Catholic Church were a factor in their decision to stop attending Mass. For most of these, simply knowing that such things had occurred, especially in parishes or with individuals known to them, was sufficient to rock their faith. A smaller number, however, relate how they were themselves the objects of abuse.

Reports of Abuse and Cover-Up

A great many respondents mentioned, if often briefly, repeated revelations concerning abuse as a factor, often alongside many others, either in their ceasing to practice or confirming them in their decision.

About 15 years ago, after various scandals involving priests, and their cover-ups etcetera, locally, nationally and worldwide, I left because I couldn't stomach what was going on. Having been an educator and protector of children, I couldn't believe how the institution had felt itself more important than the human beings it was supposed to serve. (female, 64)

I struggled with reading of child abuse within the Church and deliberate cover-ups by high-ranking clergy. (female, 73)

Understandably, where abuse came to light in parishes familiar to respondents or related to persons—either as perpetrator or victim, and in some cases both—they knew, this could have a particularly devastating effect:

I used to go and take our children regularly. However, like many people, I have felt betrayed by the (not only Catholic) Church's attitude to the seemingly countless acts of abuse, especially since the parish priest of [X] was convicted....It made me feel very uncomfortable going into the church thinking of all the children he had baptized and given sacraments to, and it made me wonder if any of the past priests were abusers too. This is especially painful since I was baptised in this same church. I received my First Communion, Confirmation and was married there 37 years ago. My parents' funerals were held there. (female, 58)

Two respondents remark movingly about how much they had hitherto admired the priests in question:

I discovered several awful truths about things that had happened in our small parish....A priest of whom we were all very in awe, and who we trusted with our children, committed suicide while awaiting trial for his sexual abuse with children, including our son's friend and several others....How could anyone knowing all that, carry on going to Mass and not stand up and shout about it?...The result is that our lives are spoilt as we had many good friends through going to Mass and now they are all rather distant. Also, we had a faith which has gone, and it affects our lives, present and future. (male, 69)

The most inspiring of these young priests was one who was deeply committed to social causes and who later became my mother's parish priest (not in this diocese), completely revitalising the area, inspiring young and old to participate in the community. He was an extraordinarily powerful force for good. However, in the last few years, he was twice convicted of serious sexual crimes against boys, some committed during that period. I struggle to make sense of this. I mention it because, having lapsed earlier in life, he was one of the forces that drew me back to the Catholic Church, and which is now a reason for my feeling it irrelevant. I pray for him. (female, 63)

Victims and Survivors

For some men, it was their own experiences of physical or sexual abuse as a child or teenager that led to their distancing from the Church.[5] The nature and gravity of what they had undergone was, in several cases, only recognized retrospectively.

Having attended a school run by priests in the 1980s, I now find it difficult to trust a priest not to harm me. (male, 48)

The past came back to haunt me when the pedophile crimes in the Church were exposed. The word "grooming" came up, and that's what had happened to me. I was abused as an 11-year-old boy by a teaching brother who made me very frightened, and when I refused to participate again he became very nasty. I was sickened

---

5. It is worth noting here that the survey was (and respondents were explicitly told that it was) anonymous, and contact details for respondents were not directly collected. At the end of the survey, respondents were given the opportunity to email if they were interested either in receiving updates on the survey's findings, or if they were willing for someone from the diocese's pastoral team to contact them. This was done, however, so that names and email addresses could not be directly correlated to a given response.

by the Church's cover-ups and denials....I have no trust in the Church. (male, 76)

When I was 12 or 13 years old, I was a scout, and the troop leader was one of the younger priests. We went on a summer camp and during this time he called me to his tent and started reading rhymes from a rugby songs book and started asking very uncomfortable questions about what some of the words meant etcetera. I said that I didn't like what was happening, and he sent me back to the tent. Later, when I was in my late teens, I spoke to some of my friends at the time, and they told me that he had molested them, not only at the camp but on other occasions. When I was in my late twenties and married, I saw that he had been arrested in America for acts against boys. (male, 58)

Among female respondents, emotional traumas of their convent or school education by nuns were cited:

I attended a primary Catholic school and a secondary grammar convent school run by nuns. They were not always kind and respectful and often shattered my self-esteem and that of the children I was friends with. I found some of them almost cruel. (female, 53)

I had been in therapy regarding the cruelty and abuse I suffered as a child and came to the realization that the way I was treated by some of the nuns at my boarding school was basically evil and not, in fact, deserved by me as a child. (female, 48)

I was taught by nuns in the 1950s. While some were angels, others made me feel very inferior and scared; my time at that primary school was hell. That is the reason I never brought my children up as Catholics and stopped going to Mass when I could. (female, 67)

CONCLUSION

So far, we have explored the main "practical and experiential" reasons, broadly conceived, that participants in the "MyStoryShared" survey identified as being of significance in their journeys of departure. Clearly our individual subthemes are by no means mutually exclusive. Very few respondents cited only a single factor, and indeed, extracts from a single participant's "story" have sometimes been quoted in two or more different sections. Also note that even where the same collection of themes recurs in different respondents' narratives, they are not necessarily weighted equally in each one.

These observations are worth considering as we move now into the second chapter, which focuses on intellectual, doctrinal, and moral reasons for Catholics' ceasing to practice. Please note that in dividing our thematic treatment up in this way, we do not mean to imply that our respondents may themselves be equally so divided. Practical/experiential and intellectual/doctrinal/moral issues are rarely so easily separated.

2

WHY?—INTELLECTUAL, DOCTRINAL, AND MORAL REASONS

The first chapter concentrated on the wide range of "practical and experiential reasons" that our respondents gave for becoming distant from the Church. Here our attention turns to matters of intellectual conviction. Half of our respondents either agreed or strongly agreed with the following statement: "I stopped believing in Catholic teaching." Naturally, this includes a broad range of possibilities, including questions concerning the existence and nature of God and reality, historical judgments regarding the nature (and conduct) of the Church, and specific views on doctrinal and moral matters. As already noted, the topical division drawn between these first two chapters is by no means hard and fast. Many of the testimonies quoted in the foregoing pages touched upon, sometimes quite heavily, matters of doctrine. Likewise, many of those quoted here will incorporate important personal or experiential factors. This will be most obvious with certain moral issues. As we will note, it is often the case that disagreements with what the Church teaches, and/or how that teaching is applied, only become "activated" as potential triggers for leaving when the point becomes a personal one too.

Again, we have structured this chapter in terms of general themes, which in most cases admit of further subdivisions. Our overarching themes are the following:

1. Philosophical and Historical Doubts

2. Doctrinal and Moral Problems

3. Vatican II and Liberalization

While the focus, here, will be on elaborating the problems respondents had with specific philosophical, moral, and doctrinal issues, it is worth noting the broader message of their responses. For some people, the message can be summed up in the words of one respondent: "I would like to be considered able to think for myself rather than be told what to believe" (male, 52). And for two others: "I do not believe in dogmatic belief systems" (male, 64), and "I disagree with the Church's claim to exclusive truth [and] its authoritarian nature" (male, 60).

With several respondents, however, the main complaint was not so much about what the Church believes and teaches, but rather its failure to explain and communicate *why* it does. Interestingly, this was most often a criticism made by younger respondents:

There's lots of stuff that's not explained and the ways of trying to do it are rubbish. (female, 18)

Apart from the Mass, very little often goes on....Education and faith building at the parish level is usually weak and sometimes those doing it probably shouldn't be. It always amazes me that people who don't agree with certain things can push [their agenda] in such contexts and get away with it. The Church really is punitive in this regard. If it were a business, some of these parish leaders would really be brand killers. Why they don't either align or move on amazes me more, but such is human behavior and the power of routine. (male, 23)

Parish life doesn't help people grow and engage with their faith.... People who undermine what the Church teaches are given positions within parishes. The diocese doesn't ensure that the people teaching and supporting young people in parishes have the correct skills or beliefs. Far too much is assumed and not checked. (female, 20)

I feel the Catholic Church has not done a good job with formation and have found this frustrating. There wasn't any established avenue or resource from the Church to support the period in my life [when I was at university]. I felt the Church offered a structure to practice but there wasn't anywhere to explore, question, or engage. After Confirmation, there isn't anything, at least not on any large scale, to help people deal with the challenges and questions of life. There wasn't any sense of cohesive parish life, faith building, or spirituality groups or support. (male, 34)

PHILOSOPHICAL AND HISTORICAL DOUBTS

As already quoted from some of the testimonies from those who stopped attending Mass regularly as young adults, some Catholics simply stop believing in God—or at least stop believing in his existence strongly enough to still feel compelled to go to Mass. Those offering grounds for this tend to cite either scientific explanations as undercutting the rationality of theistic belief or issues of evil and suffering.

Now I wonder if God really exists. I believe God was once used to explain phenomena which is now explained by science. (male, 37)

I lost my faith through studying science at school and beginning to think for myself about the plausibility of the existence of God and the context in which religions were established. I concluded that Christianity, being 2000 years old, was just a cultural creation based on beliefs held by people 2000 years ago when they didn't have explanations for seemingly divine occurrences. (male, 29)

In all honesty, I feel that religion is a somewhat outdated notion, and now that we have such scientific advances we no longer need a higher being to explain how we came to be on this Earth. I now put my faith in science. (female, 18)

I found belief in a God made in man's image impossible to sustain. The thought that the creator of countless galaxies, stars, planets would be worried if I slept with a woman (or a man) outside marriage or missed Mass on Sunday is just not sustainable. (male, 68)

I started meeting people who didn't have my [Catholic] background. People who had been damaged by violent parents, a violent society. I began to realize that these people didn't have my perceptions or resources, and that their choices were therefore limited. So, I began to realize that "free choice" is really a fallacy. Sometimes people I met were so damaged that they did things that got them into trouble....I painfully realized that no matter how much I prayed, solutions would never present themselves. I had to find my own solutions for my own problems, but I could not solve the problems of the world through prayer or any other means....I realized that there was no God to save people....So, my God died a horrible, painful death. I suffered more with this loss than any broken heart, and kept hoping it wasn't true, so I was open to new explanations, insights, etc., but the arguments were too weak and irrational. (female, 54)

While the latter respondent was by no means alone in expressing a sense of sorrow in this regard, others were less bothered or, as in the second excerpt below, felt that they ought to be.

I finally realized none of you believe in it, and if you don't, why would I? (female, 49)

I've made friends who are agnostic at best and discussed my faith with them. When I try to justify my belief in a supernatural being or Christ as a felt presence in my life, I feel silly. For really the first time in my life, my doubts outweigh my faith. I went to Mass on Easter Sunday this year, hoping that I would be able to make some connection to Christ, but felt nothing. It saddened me that I'd gone from a lazy or lapsed Catholic to an agnostic but felt guilty for feeling sad. To be blunt, I don't feel guilty about not believing in Santa Claus. (male, 35)

For a handful of respondents, it was not so much general doubts about God, but more specific doubts about the origins and/or authority of the Christian tradition itself.

Once I read more into church history, and the late origins of many Roman Catholic positions and doctrines, I could not maintain a consistent position as a Traditional Catholic, since I realized that the Tridentine traditions I was defending are simply an earlier set of innovations, which look shaky considering the practices and canons of the Church pre-schism. (male, 27)

I came to a profound realization that Christianity was a cultural expression arising from historical circumstances, and that any metaphysical or spiritual claims it made were a form of wishful thinking—we made god in our own image, so to speak. It was relatively shocking, but it "felt" right. I have read and researched a lot in the time since this "conversion," on both sides of the debate. I am still deeply interested in religions and cultures. I do not feel any sense of loss; more a sense of relief and freedom. (male, 42)

DOCTRINAL AND MORAL PROBLEMS

All respondents were asked to state the extent to which certain "controversial" issues were a factor in distancing themselves from the Church. (The categories offered were based on the ones asked

in the Diocese of Springfield, Illinois, survey; see Hardy et al. 2014.[1])
Their responses are summarized in figure 2.

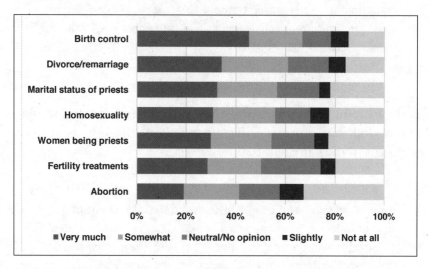

Figure 2. Breakdown of "MyStoryShared" responses to the following question:
"From this list of issues and policies, please select whether one or more of these
was a reason for distancing yourself from the Catholic Church."

Elsewhere in the survey, respondents were asked to elaborate
more generally on any beliefs or practices specific to the Catholic
Church that troubled them. In many cases, these had already been
mentioned, frequently in detail. Perhaps not surprisingly, matters
of marriage, sexual ethics, and life concerns featured prominently—
although, as we will note, not exclusively—here. As mentioned previously, these are all cases where "doctrinal disagreement" is not an
abstract affair, but rather impacts itself most forcefully on people's
personal, intimate lives.

In the following subsections, we cover each of the main, recurrent doctrinal and moral issues raised by our respondents in some
detail. These do not, however, constitute an exhaustive list. Over

---

1. For purposes of comparison, we felt that it was important to replicate the
precise language used, which we did (hence "issues and policies"). In *presenting*
this data, however, we have omitted the category "the Bible." Although our
respondents were indeed asked that question, we do not feel that it was sufficiently
transparent in meaning, either to our participants or to us as researchers,
especially when framed in terms of an "issue" or "policy," to yield any usable data.

the course of 256 individual submissions, disagreements with a great many specific doctrines and practices were mentioned. These included the veneration shown to Mary, the virgin birth, the immaculate conception, the real presence of Christ in the Eucharist, the assumption, purgatory, use of statues and relics, original sin, and indulgences. Most of these were mentioned only once, and then only in passing, and often as part of a longer list of things with which a person disagreed. In other words, none of these appear to have played a significant role in a respondent's distancing from the Church, except as part of an accumulated list of "things I don't accept."

The topics we explore are different in that each of them does appear to have played an important direct or indirect role in at least some respondents' ceasing to practice. In the following subsections, we take each of the most common topics in turn (although, in practice, these often overlap). In common with our policy throughout this book, which we consider proper to a "listening exercise" such as this, we will "share" our respondents' own "stories" at face value. In other words, we seek to offer an accurate record of the reasons nonpracticing Catholics *themselves* give for how this has come about. Of course, quotation does not imply endorsement.

Divorce and Remarriage

As is clear from figure 2, church teaching on divorce/remarriage was cited by a majority of our sample as being very much or somewhat a reason for distancing themselves from the Church. Moreover, elsewhere in the survey, just under one in ten referred to the status of their marriage as the main cause of their ceasing to practice. The specifics of everyone's situation are varied. Not for nothing, indeed, did Pope Francis recently affirm Saint John Paul II's observation that "there is no family that does not know how selfishness, discord, tension, and conflict violently attack and at times mortally wound its own communion: hence there arise many and varied forms of division in family life" (*Amoris Laetitia* 106; quoting *Familiaris Consortio* 21).

Experiences of divorce and/or remarriage (either their own, or their partner's, or not infrequently both) were common. So, too, were accompanying feelings of frustration and injustice.

My marriage broke down and I went through a difficult time. I met a new partner and was highly aware this is contrary to the Church's teachings and, as a result, feel quite removed from the Church. (female, 38)

My marriage broke down, and I lost my faith so I stopped taking Communion. It was hard to go to church and see my wife and child there. I still go sometimes, but don't participate in the Mass. (male, 60)

I attended church every week until a few years after I married a divorcé. Having been raised a Catholic from birth and never having married until I married my husband, I find it very hard to understand why I should be denied the sacrament of Communion just because I married. I was further discouraged from attending church when the parish priest spoke about marriage bringing people closer to the Church. When I said that marriage was taking me away from the Church, his reply was to say he recognized that there were victims out there. I do not see myself as a victim. (female, 59)

Until my early 20s, I followed the Catholic tradition with fervor and conviction. Then I had to choose between remaining within the Church or marrying a deeply spiritual partner, who had been divorced. We were told that we would not be permitted to marry within the Church, even though he had never been a member of any church and had never been baptized. (female, 65)

I gave up Catholicism when I was 33, a single parent, with a new relationship. The single parent bit was OK until I got a new partner. My marriage had been to a divorced man, so I suppose in the eyes of the Catholic Church I have never been married. That seems to me like formalism. (female, 68)

I was let down by the Catholic Church...when I married my husband. I fell in love with a man who was separated from his wife....My father, a very devout Catholic, talked to me and said he would ask some priests he knew if they would be willing to give us a blessing as we all knew we would not be welcome in church. After asking four different priests, only one said he would offer us a blessing but it would have to be in private after our wedding. It was at this time that I felt that I lost my faith because I was being treated like I had done something wrong. (female, 35)

Although some respondents mentioned the existence of the annulment process, few felt that this was something that they either could or should embark upon. This could be for several reasons.

I married a divorced man and the church I approached, the place where I had celebrated both my First Holy Communion and Confirmation, refused to marry us, but the priest did say he would give us a blessing. He explained I would need to get his marriage annulled. He had two children. I could not, and would not, do that. (female, 58)

I approached a priest (not my parish priest) for some guidance on applying for a marriage annulment. His advice was to go and find another church to attend as I was probably causing a scandal in my own parish as I continue to take communion....I also spoke to a Jesuit priest who told me that marriage was a contract—one which it would appear my husband broke when he refused his role as an equal parent. But I have no access to annulment unless I declare I married in error or didn't love my ex-husband when I got married, i.e., that the marriage was not valid. Not so—he just changed the rules of engagement and I was left to deal with the aftermath. (female, 57)

I did all I could to save my marriage. I sought advice, I was prepared to forgive for [my husband's] affair, etc., but he refused to do anything to save our marriage and respect the vows we made. It angers me that, in the eyes of the Church, I am still "classed" as a married woman! Through no fault of my own and not through my doing I am now divorced. Who is the Catholic Church to tell me I am still wed when legally I am not? I discussed annulment with the priest, but he did not encourage it and advised that it is a very long journey to take—another punishment for not remaining married! (female, 47)

In fact, for one woman who *did* undergo the process of seeking an annulment, this became the cause of not just her, but also her children, leaving the Church.

During the annulment process, I felt very unsupported and conflicted....I needed the support not just of the priests but also of congregation members who were friends. It made me feel as if I had been judged and excluded....The process is secretive and takes ages....The relationship and the marriage were over, but we are still Catholic parents of these children. There was no effort from the Church to respond....I stopped going to church because I can't reconcile the talk about compassion and family with the [lack of support for] families with real responses when relationships are under stress. My oldest child now sees herself as a Buddhist in principle and my second child refused to be confirmed and told me she will never marry in the Catholic Church because of my experience....I tend to go when I am alone and need to feel connected to other people. (female, 54)

Two divorced and remarried respondents wrote movingly of their sorrow at no longer being able to receive holy communion (although it must be noted that neither respondent expresses *disagreement* with the Church's teaching).

Now I am not allowed to receive Holy Eucharist...as this is the "heart" of the Mass—it is too painful to watch everyone else "receiving"—but I am not able to. So, I don't go anymore. (female, 36)

My greatest need is to be able to receive Holy Communion: I have received the Body and Blood of Christ on three or four occasions; outside of my own church but have been filled with guilt because Catholic doctrine forbids divorcés from receiving Holy Communion. I am unclear of what God expects of me in terms of repentance. (male, 60)

As it happens, confusion was a common reaction of respondents. A number referred to having received conflicting advice from priests vis-à-vis receiving the Eucharist.

After having remarried, I asked the parish priest if I could attend Mass and take the sacraments. He confirmed that I could. My (second) wife and our young son attended; both were baptized into the Church. My wife was confirmed at the same time; the ceremonies were both on Easter Saturday. It was a wonderful time. During the last year, our new parish priest announced from the altar that many who took the sacrament of Holy Communion were actually not allowed. He specified those who should not accept the sacrament, amongst which were those who are divorced and remarried. I felt that, clearly, I do not have a place within the Church and should not attend Mass. The consequence is that neither does my wife or young son who, aged nine, should have some religious connection to the Church, or at least a church. (male, 69)

47

I was married 15 years ago. It's my first marriage but my husband was married before in a registry office, as was our marriage. I have asked a few priests what that means regarding my status with the Church and their views have been varied. From "once a Catholic, always a Catholic and you can receive communion" to "you can't receive communion" and felt ostracized. (female, 52)

Sex outside Marriage

Divorce and remarriage was not, in fact, the only matrimony-related problem that had come up for our respondents. Sometimes these revealed themselves in quite ordinary ways. Several parents found themselves conflicted about Church teaching on marriage when seeing their grown-up children live with partners to whom they are committed but not married.

When my adult children started to date and had long-term partners but were not married, I found this difficult. Their behavior was very normal among their peers and I consider them to be good people, but they were at odds with Church teaching. (female, 57)

Several other (often younger) respondents simply felt that the Church's stance on such matters was outdated and irrelevant.

The religious practice that sex must occur between a man and a woman after they have married is an archaic mode of thinking and goes against the freedom of two people expressing their love for each other. (male, 24)

Marriage and starting families are now not a priority for young adults in relationships and such teachings alienate this demographic. (female, 25)

Rather different are those respondents for whom the problem lies not in the Church's strictures, per se, but rather in their own failures to live up to them:

I am in a relationship with the man I live with. It was a relationship that began before I started going back to church. He encouraged me to try to reintegrate that part of myself. He used to come to church with me for a while. Then it reached a stage, however, where he didn't want to get "more religious," and although we haven't argued about it, there is now an awkwardness around this subject....I have never married and have never had children. Both things are a matter of regret and sorrow, and I can see that they spring from choices I have made and paths I have walked....I am stuck. I have never lived as a Roman Catholic adult. I don't know what that would be like. When I was a teenager, I felt like it would be too hard to keep the rules. Now, with much of life lived, I can see how those "rules" may have supported me....I no longer regard myself as Catholic because I do respect the parameters the Church has set up, and I am living outside them. (female, 42)

Having committed adultery, which ended a 25-year marriage, with four children, I immediately resigned my position [as altar server and Extraordinary Minister of Holy Communion] with my church. A deep sense of loss ensued, but I knew there would be little sympathy/understanding from parishioners for my wrongdoing, and even less from the clergy. I attempted Confession on possibly three or four occasions over a period of approximately two years; each time with a different priest. Only one priest gave any recognition to my position and conveyed (through God) forgiveness of my sins. The mixed messages from clergy, my sense of abandonment from the Church, and my own feelings of guilt led me to stop attending Sunday Mass, where I would hide at the back of the church. I stopped attending Mass for approximately two to three years before I eventually felt that God was not completely abandoning me and so I began to attend weekday Mass. (male, 60)

LGBT Issues

The Catholic position on homosexuality was raised, in numerous ways, by many respondents. Given that legislation in the United Kingdom permitting same-sex partners to be civilly married had come into force in March 2014, only eighteen months before the survey opened, it is not surprising that this issue was often cited.

For some respondents, the Church's approach to those attracted to the same-sex was a very personal issue. For these respondents, it was often a decisive factor in their having left the Church.

Ten years ago, I came to terms with my homosexuality and felt that the Church was unwelcoming to me and other people like me. (male, 56)

I feel I have to hide this part of myself and no longer feel welcomed or accepted by the Church. I can't imagine how painful it must be for young people who know they are gay to attend Church. (female, 53)

I am a lesbian, and therefore, obviously, I cannot agree with teachings on same-sex relationships. (female, 51)

I am a gay man. The barrage of anti-gay propaganda from the Church made me feel irredeemable. The final straw was Cardinal [X]'s speech in Valletta, Malta, in which he said people campaigning for gay equality (not marriage!) were no better than the Nazis who bombed Valletta during the war. My dad was on a ship that was bombed in the Port of Valletta. I bitterly resent being placed in the same category as those who bombed him. (male, 71)

Other respondents wrote,

I disagree with the belief that the practice of homosexuality is disordered, especially when a good proportion of men in the Church are gay and suffering in silence. (female, 64)

Jesus would be appalled at how the Church talks about homosexuals. The current Pope has tried to speak about this issue, however, when there is a new Pope, we will be back to the point where I have to apologize to my "liberal" friends for being a Catholic. (male, 35)

I find the doctrine that homosexuality is disordered very troubling. I have several gay friends, both men and women, and can testify that there is nothing disordered about them or their lives. What is disordered is dishonesty and misuse in sexual relationships, and heterosexual people are as likely to be guilty of this as homosexual people. We are all human and we all need help to live honest intimate lives. Some people are gay. Everyone needs to get used to that. (female, 38)

I know you all think that homosexuality is a sin, but I just don't understand why, if someone is a good person and is kind and lives a good Christian life, they should be penalized. (female, 24)

People are people, and it makes me angry that a religion claiming to be loving and living like Jesus excludes people because of who they love. (female, 30)

I had the misfortune of listening to a homily in which a priest made the analogy that gay marriage "is like a woman marrying her dog." Simply horrible—am I to encourage my children to listen to such hatred? No, not while there is breath in my body. (female, 37)

The Catholic Church needs to be representative of the time in which we live. Jesus was a changemaker and dared to challenge the old ways in his time. We should be doing the same now. (female, 50)

In addition to the issue of homosexuality, a small number of respondents wrote about their concern regarding the Church's stance on gender issues.

There are children born that are not obviously male or female and have to have their gender assigned to them, sometimes even having surgery as children to make them fit the gender given at birth. These children sometimes grow up and feel that they have been assigned to the wrong sex. This happens; we are all made in the image of God, therefore there cannot be anything wrong in people wishing to have gender reassignment if that is how they feel they should be....The Church needs more scientists, especially biologists and geneticists to help it understand the natural world and what we are made of. (female, 53)

Fertility and Life Issues

When prompted, most participants affirmed that Church teachings on birth control had been "very much" or "somewhat" a reason to distance themselves from the Church (see figure 2). Interestingly, however, earlier in the survey, when providing detailed responses to the (deliberately nondirective) invitation to narrate what had changed between "a time in your life when you attended

Mass on a more regular basis" and "now," the subject was brought up by only a very small number. One explanation of this might be that, while a considerable proportion of the sample disagreed with Catholic teaching on the topic, therefore forming part of a "cumulative" estrangement from the Church, for only a few was it a decisive factor. Recall, too, as already noted in the introduction, the precise age profile of our survey sample. That is, only a relatively small proportion of our respondents were adults when Pope Paul VI promulgated *Humanae Vitae*, reiterating the longstanding Christian prohibition on artificial birth control, in 1968.

Nevertheless, the Church's opposition to contraception was often brought up by respondents, if only briefly.

> I feel alienated by some of the teachings of the Catholic Church, which seem out-of-date, especially *Humanae Vitae*. (male, 43)
>
> I think it's time the Catholic Church reassessed its stance on contraception. With an ever-expanding population and AIDS, I believe it is irresponsible to continue to dictate this teaching. (female, 45)
>
> The Church gives the impression that you aren't capable of regulating your own fertility. (male, 68)

For one respondent, the paucity of large families among Catholics was proof that "everyone is using something" (female, 54), and thus that the Church is out of touch with its own members. Others were mystified and/or expressed incredulity at the Church's stance.

> I love my wife and am faithful to her. We are best friends. We do not want children so use contraception. So, I need to go to Confession and apologize for this. To be honest, it's such nonsense that, in fact, it doesn't push me away from the Church. Some Catholic doctrine I feel you can ignore without being a bad

Catholic. Jesus doesn't strike me as a man who would "tut-tut" over contraception. (male, 35)

Preventing conception is totally different from destroying life after conception which some birth control methods do. The Church should differentiate. (female, 61)

I cannot understand the Church's teaching on contraception—what is the problem with barrier methods which prevent contact between egg and sperm so no conception and no embryo? I can understand the argument against the coil which prevents implantation of a fertilized embryo/potential human being but lumping them together under one ban is ludicrous. There are significant differences and completely different theological arguments regarding what happens in these two types of contraception (barrier method versus coil), and the Church's refusal to allow discussion about this is very counterproductive. All my many current, lapsed and ex-Catholic friends use a form of contraception, most of them the pill or a barrier method. They cannot, like me, see what the theological argument is against this type of prevention of conception. We are all educated and can see and understand the difference between preventing conception in the first place and preventing implantation of a fertilized embryo/potential person. (female, 53)

Interestingly, no respondent betrayed any awareness of, still less experience with, forms of natural family planning (or natural fertility awareness), which the Church permits and, in theory, promotes for the practice of responsible parenthood.[2]

---

2 For example, "If therefore there are well-grounded reasons for spacing births, arising from the physical or psychological condition of husband or wife, or from external circumstances, the Church teaches that married people may then take advantage of the natural cycles immanent in the reproductive system and engage in marital intercourse only during those times that are infertile" (*Humanae Vitae* 16). The National Health Service's own advice on natural family planning can be found at http://www.nhs.uk/Conditions/contraception-guide/Pages/natural -family-planning.aspx (accessed March 7, 2016).

For one respondent, it was not the Church's opposition to certain means of avoiding pregnancy, but rather its condemnation of certain means of achieving it that were a very personal problem.

> Not long after we were married in the Catholic Church (my husband is Baptist), we discovered that we were unable to have children naturally. We chose to go down an IVF route. I have never felt so alone and abandoned in my life because of this decision by the Catholic Church. I simply don't know anymore where I fit into the life of the Church. The very few priests I have spoken to about this have been very judgmental, and I'm simply at a loss in my relationship with the Church. My faith is strong and, to be honest, it is the main thing that has got me through this very painful experience. We are attending an Anglican church where we feel more welcomed and less judged. As a married Catholic woman who is unable to have children, there simply is no place for me in such a family-focused Church. (female, 39)

From our list of common "hot button" issues that might have distanced respondents from Catholicism, the Church's condemnation of abortion was the one least identified as being either "very much" or "somewhat" a factor (see figure 2). Meanwhile, a third of our sample said that it was "not at all" a factor, the highest proportion across all the categories. Nevertheless, those for whom the Church's pro-life stance was an issue clearly regarded it as a significant one.

> Being pro-life is an old-fashioned idealism. If someone is not able to raise a child properly into the world, they shouldn't have to—it's unfair on that child. (female, 28)
>
> I remain a Catholic who believes in abortion rights for women, though I can never say it, because in my opinion people get completely hysterical about the subject. (female, 53)

> Although I do not agree with abortion, I do feel that under certain circumstances women should have the option. (female, 35)

For two women who had had abortions themselves, this was understandably a particularly sensitive topic:

> Catholicism has let me down so much. When I needed it to be there, I was condemned and judged (for having an abortion). (female, 40)
>
> I am Catholic in my heart and sometimes feel angry and upset that I no longer feel welcome within the Catholic Church. My ex-husband made me have an abortion, and I then divorced him. With those two crosses against my name, I don't feel that I can now step in a Catholic Church. (female, 43)

The Priesthood

Approximately a third of respondents stated that the reason for distancing themselves from the Church was "very much" influenced by the fact women cannot be ordained as priests. A similar proportion of respondents said the same about "the marital status of priests," which was presumably understood to mean the normativity of priestly celibacy within the Latin Church.[3] While both referring to the priesthood, these issues are, of course, separate. And

---

3. This is a complicated area to capture accurately in a single phrase on a questionnaire. The ordination of married men to the priesthood is a perfectly normal feature within many, though not all, of the "Eastern Catholic Churches" in full communion with Rome (although even in these Churches, married men cannot become bishops). In the Latin Church, however, a celibate priesthood has been the norm for many centuries, although, even here, there are exceptions, most notably, for former Anglican clergy.

indeed, among those respondents who chose to elaborate on the topic, the reasons for objecting were very different.

Regarding the nonordination of women, this often formed one part of a broader, and more widespread, expression of dismay or disgust with the Church's perceived treatment of women.

> The Church is guilty of the subjugation of women. This stems from the age-old fear of men who know, ultimately, that they can't function without women as they cannot give birth and so subjugate them out of fear....The Catholic doctrine is still to subvert women's rights and see women as subservient to men, when in fact, men are responsible for most of the ills of this world. (male, 76)
>
> I disagree with the idea that women aren't equal to men and shouldn't be in positions of power. This is classic misogyny which is all about sexual competition and choice of mates. (male, 26)
>
> I am a woman in my 50s with my own business, and I simply cannot support a Church which is still sidelining women in so obvious a way. (female, 52)

Based on these and similar objections, some respondents felt that the Church ought to be ordaining women.

> Male-only priests is killing the church. The men who are becoming priests tend to be a little odd, and perhaps more fundamentalist—which should not be encouraged. A new, young priest in our parish comes in frilly frocks and 1950s priests' hats. What is that about?! (female, 52)
>
> Yes, I agree that there is a gender difference, and that men and women have complementary strengths and talents. It is how this is talked about, and how it is lived out that troubles me. I don't

think, however, that it is at all helpful to humanity to define a person's role according to their gender. I think some women would make good priests, just as some men make good religious. In the family, it is not helpful to have rigidly defined gender roles. It is more helpful to children to see their parents celebrating their strengths, wherever these lie, and working together as a team. The way that gender difference is emphasized in the Catholic Church, or maybe the way it is lived out, seems to encourage subservience in some women and arrogance in some men. Having witnessed my own mother's subservience and sense of unworthiness, even though she has lived by all the rules, I would say that her womanhood was not fully supported, or her flourishing facilitated by the Church, and this is incredibly sad. In addition, there are things about gender which we do not yet understand, and which defy current definitions. (female, 42)

By contrast, as one noted, the "enforced celibacy of clergy" (male, 60) attracted fewer explicit critics. Interestingly, while proponents for women priests tended to argue on the positive basis of either the rights or merits of women, the case for married priests was primarily a negative one. This was often framed in terms of the failings of celibate priests.

The fact that priests are not able to marry, I feel, attracts some that hide in that role. I feel a priest that is married could add a lot more to his parish life with a wife supporting him. (female, 56)

I am still of the opinion that if priests could marry or have fulfilled relationships, there would be no or very little pedophilia. (male, 58)

The celibacy of priests is unnatural and leads to the possibility of scandal. (female, 38)

VATICAN II
AND LIBERALIZATION

In general, it is fair to say that a sizable proportion of the above-quoted criticisms of doctrinal and moral positions—and how they are applied—are motivated by a sense that the Catholic Church should, or indeed must, become more "liberal" or "progressive." In other words, the Church should bring its formal teachings more into line with the ethical and cultural norms prevalent in Britain today. For many of our respondents, the Church's views on homosexual relationships, contraception, marriage, or "women in general," are simply "behind the times," "backward," and "outdated." This overall pattern is not surprising and is consistent with all other such qualitative studies in this area.

Nevertheless, this is by no means the whole story. In common with other studies (e.g., Hoge et al. 1981, 124–29), our sample included a significant "minority report" from those critical of what they regard to be a deleterious liberalization, or at least dilution, of authentic Catholic teaching and practice. In this area, as in all others, respondents exhibit significant diversity. In chapter 1, we discussed concerns regarding a loss of sacredness and tradition in the liturgy specifically. Often, however, such complaints were symptomatic of a more wide-ranging malaise. For instance:

> The Church is too liberal, too man-centered, not God-centered; too "touchy feely," not orthodox. Poor liturgy, the sacrifice of the Mass seems to have been compromised. (male, 56)

For several such respondents, the root causes of these problems were ascribed to the wide-ranging changes that occurred in Catholic life in the decades following the Second Vatican Council (1962–65). Here, a prominent theme is that it was the Church they had loved (and, indeed, still do) that had changed, and not they themselves.

From the late 70s, I attended Mass less and less until about 1990. I was of the generation where I was a teenager during Vatican II. I found the early seventies a challenging time as everything was up in the air. It was a time where my faith, in the Church at least, started to die away....There was an attitude, by priests and others, that people like myself needed to "get with the spirit of the times" and that we weren't following the will of the church if we objected to whatever idea they decided to do (removing altar rails, moving the altar, changing the music, stopping Latin, stopping devotions, reducing access to confessions, etc.). Stuff like this happened before I stopped going. It felt like an ongoing stripping of identity— well, it really was. It was dismissive and patronizing to many in the congregation, and we had little say....I think the Church changed, I didn't. I feel disillusioned, even a bit bitter. Decline has happened, in part, because of the strategy employed by the Church since the late sixties. It was a big time and the Church got pushed along on the surf and it seems to have hit the rocks. Is it any wonder people now fight back against the Church on doctrine, or can't be bothered? I don't blame them. Why follow a teaching and in ten years the Church changes tone or track? It's a betrayal. (female, 64)

For another respondent, a religious sister at the time of the Council, the postconciliar upheavals were particularly traumatic and ultimately caused her to leave her Order after twelve years in vows.

The changes that were pushed on us by leadership teams in the wake of Vatican II in our Orders were painful and distressing. Thousands of us left feeling that our sense of calling and vocation had been attacked and gutted by a liberal revision and takeover. I have felt lost ever since I left, but I knew I couldn't stay in that environment. The Church leadership offered us little to no acknowledgement for the trouble they had inflicted on us, or for the work we had done, or that was being lost. The Church, in its

> madness, has driven away plenty. The self-deception, to a considerable extent, still goes on. The recent celebration of the event that has caused so much suffering and decline says it all. The Church should apologize to the people it has hurt and admit its mistakes. (female, 64)

She adds, "I [still] regard myself as Catholic, but have since made the Orthodox Church my spiritual home."

Concerns like these were not only found among those who had lived through the postconciliar changes. Similar issues were raised, in some detail, by respondents in their twenties and early thirties. For instance:

> Sadly, my feeling is that Catholicism has been undermined for decades, and this has caused fatigue and confusion for many faithful Catholics. Bishops need to support the clerics so that they can follow papal decrees and teach the faith, ancient and living, correctly with the empowerment of orthodox laity. Stop giving time to those who seek a step-by-step dismantling of the Church. If the Church looks confused, seems to change when the pressure mounts, or fudges on difficult issues, then it's not attractive to anyone. (female, 23)

> My concern is the increasing liberalization of Catholicism that takes it away from the strength provided by the beautiful traditions and culture. Strangely, it seems to be going the same way as the Anglican church, even though the Anglican church too has already alienated many of its members. It is watering down its teachings to please people in the short term and thereby losing what is special and true about the faith, and thus less able to sustain people spiritually in the longer term. This may seem like a small issue, but it has truly broken the hearts of thousands of ordinary people who are expected to forget or dismiss the teachings they were brought

> up with and adapt to new ideas. This is not Catholicism....It is not the fault of the people if they don't have knowledge of the faith—although it is all too easy to blame them—it is the fault of those who are continuing to fail to teach and pass these traditions on. (female, 33)

Finally, considering theological attention recently given to this topic (Martin 2012; Bullivant and Arredondo 2017, 11–30), it is noteworthy that several respondents singled out a downplaying of sin, and hence complacency concerning salvation, as having especially undermined the Church's mission.

> Everyone goes to heaven regardless if you are Catholic or not, what is the point of being Catholic? (male, 24)
>
> The lack of focus on transformation, or penance, was an issue. Often parishes would give less than an hour a week for Confession (or before Mass). Who can approach it in that manner without support and teaching? We had a priest who felt we should have a public absolution instead, and so reduced access times for Confession. No doubt the lack of participation was used to support his point. Who would attend if they've also been told for twenty years "it's all good" and sin/repentance is an old concept? Many people gave up, even if they didn't leave. (female, 64)

CONCLUSION

Throughout this chapter, our findings show varying and overlapping reasons for why our participants stopped attending Mass or left the Church entirely. If there is any one conclusion to be drawn from this, it is that there is no single "silver bullet"—one thing or coherent set of things—that the Church might change, were it even possible, to prevent more such people leaving or returning (though on the latter subject, see chapter 3). Nevertheless, several general patterns emerge.

For example, what recurs often throughout the 256 accounts is a long, gradual process of "accumulating dissatisfaction." In other words, many respondents report, directly or indirectly, that prior to an actual "break" with attending Mass, there was a significant period of feeling not at home, albeit for assorted reasons, or else of going because one always has. In such situations, a disruption of the status quo (e.g., leaving for university, or perhaps one's children doing so; moving to a new parish; a period of illness), or a single unpleasant experience with a member of the parish, often triggers the decision to stop attending. With no deep, intrinsic reasons keeping them there, instead of trying to find a new parish or Mass time or over-coming whatever difficulty there is, they simply stop going. Of course, this is not true in all cases. But over half of our respondents felt that ceasing to attend Mass was a gradual process.

In the closing chapter, where we offer some pastoral recom-mendations, we will return to some of these issues. In the following two chapters, however, as well as asking our respondents why they left, we also ask them respectively what they missed and what, if anything, might possibly bring them back.

3

WHAT DO THEY MISS?

Certainly, in this survey, negative impressions or experiences of and attitudes toward the Catholic Church are to be expected. In contrast, a survey targeting weekly Mass-goers, or even recent converts, would have a very different tone and emphasis. Nevertheless, even in our sample there remains much that is still attractive, impressive, and inspirational about Catholicism. While approximately one-tenth of respondents noted that there is "nothing" that still attracts them to the Church, many others expressed—and often in quite moving terms—their abiding attachment to, and affection for, various aspects of the Catholic faith.

I love the Church and I love Mass. I love the saints and the religious orders. (female, 53)

I like mysteries, devotion to angels and saints, ritual, connection with seasons/cycles of the year, candles, incense, simple prayer, rites of passage (sacraments). (female, 41)

And, intriguingly, in the words of one,

Basically, I like everything but attending. (male, 73)

Related to this is the salient fact that 49 percent of our sample noted that they still identify as Catholics, and a further 27 percent commented that they do "sometimes, but not at others."

(There was an interesting gender difference here: four-fifths of the women in our sample chose one of those options, compared to only two-thirds of the men.) For some, no doubt, their mode of "identifying" extends little beyond ticking the Catholic box on surveys every so often. For others, however, this is a core part of their sense of self. The complexities of "identity" (e.g., Appiah 2016) have been a popular topic of late, and there have been valuable studies exploring what people mean by describing themselves as "Christian" (see Day 2011), or indeed, as "Catholic" specifically (Smith et al. 2014, 126–54; Pew Research Center 2015, 22–38). Here we simply note the array of positions evidenced by our own respondents.

> Being a Catholic is part of my cultural identity. Even if I never go to Mass again I will always consider myself a Catholic. (female, 52)
>
> I think I will always be a Catholic but not necessarily a practising Catholic. (female, 70)
>
> I consider myself Catholic by upbringing and I suppose by "culture," but no longer observant. (male, 27)
>
> I consider myself lapsed but attached. (female, 51)
>
> I am proud to be a Catholic, my children have attended a Catholic school, and I was baptized and married in a Catholic church. However, I do not currently attend church or feel part of the wider "Catholic" community. (female, 45)
>
> I feel an underlying connection to the Catholic Church but am no longer a practising Catholic. I sometimes see myself as a believer, and at other times not. (female, 19)
>
> I'm proud to call myself a Catholic and would like to practise more. (female, 30)

Admittedly, other respondents were conflicted about their Catholic identity: "Almost embarrassed to admit to being Catholic" (female, 54), in the words of one person. Yet overall, this lingering feeling of belonging—even if loosely, distantly, or qualifiedly—was expressed in positive or at least neutral terms.

In this chapter, we explore the responses to the following direct question: "What things do you find attractive about the Catholic Church?" These are divided into the following different, not necessarily hard-and-fast groupings:

1. Community

2. The Mass

3. History, Culture, and Tradition

4. Charitable Outreach

5. Pope Francis

6. Other Factors

COMMUNITY

In chapter 1, we noted the considerable number of respondents who said that they were uncomfortable with the feeling of community in their parish. Several wrote movingly about their longing for community. We detailed some specific negative experiences of parish community that had been a factor in people's alienation from the Church. It is surprising, then, that approximately a third of those who wrote about what still attracts them to the Church expressed, in varying ways, that it was "a sense of community."

It was my home and refuge. (female, 45)

Although my memories of school should have put me off the Church for life, for some reason they didn't. I tried other churches, but never felt at home. I felt at home in the Catholic Church. (female, 67)

The communal dimension of the Church was often spoken of in terms of loss: something once treasured, now sadly left behind. For one fifty-three-year-old woman, the parish "used to be an extension of my family." A sixty-nine-year-old man, meanwhile, regretfully mentioned "a feeling of belonging now gone." Others recognized that church community is something still enjoyed by others, though they are no longer interested in it for themselves.

The following comments indicate the affection many still hold for parish life:

I like the sense of community and togetherness on a Sunday morning. (male, 29)

Parishioners are welcoming and friendly in almost every parish you go to. (female, 52)

I like the fact that it is generally open to all comers. This was a feature that attracted my late husband who joined the Church seven years before he died. (female, 68)

The Church and religion in general is an inclusive place and it gives people hope and something to live for when they've been in a dark place, and that's a great thing. (female, 24)

The community is central to the fond memories I have of growing up in a Catholic family. (female, 25)

My Catholic education always gave me a sense of belonging to a spiritual family and, in my opinion, an all-round and grounded upbringing. (male, 47)

Mass attendees are generally very friendly. I believe that the church in Portsmouth offers opportunities for all parishioners to participate in activities. (male, 48)

I find everyone in the Catholic Church to be friendly, helpful, and supportive, and as far as I can tell, they are all good people....I like the fact that the Church has all sorts of people who attend Mass and are happy to give up their time for this purpose. All the religious people I have known through the Church are good people too, doing their best. (male, 54)

I love community and have been lucky in living in a parish that feels like a family. I feel that the Church is moving and evolving, which is positive. I love what our parish and diocese do to encourage the young. Had this happened years earlier, my son may [have] still call[ed] himself a Catholic. (female, 50)

There are some amazing, loving, open-minded people. (male, 32)

The feeling of community—when you move around a lot with work as I used to, that can be very nice. (female, 51)

A strong parish community spirit can be a warm and welcoming thing to anyone that needs it. (female, 45)

For some respondents, their praise was not so much for parishes in general, but was reserved for a specific one with which they were acquainted.

My local parish is, and always will be "home" to me. Even when I return after a long break, I am always welcomed back and definitely feel that this parish is for me. (female, 65)

In my old parish, it was a sense of community spirit. The families of all the children at the local school attended together and enhanced the experience especially for First Communions and baptisms. (female, 50)

In recent years, visiting my sister's parish church...I have seen what the Church should be: friendly, open, and with a sense of a community sharing belief in God. There is always a happy atmosphere. (female, 51)

I felt welcomed at [X Parish]...where the priest was relaxed and did a lovely baptismal ceremony for my son years ago. I attended his Masses before and following the baptism, too, for a long time. (female, 33)

I really love my local church...which is very welcoming and inclusive, and [X school] is unbelievably amazing. (female, 45)

In some cases, this good feeling was tempered by certain qualifications. Mostly, these centered on how things *used to be* much better than they are now.

I liked the people. Not terribly pleased with the formality that seems to have returned. There seems to be some distance between clergy and laity introduced in recent years. (male, 65)

I loved the community feel of Mass; making contact each week with people; people caring for each other and rallying round when life got difficult for individuals; the parish priest being at the very center of the community and encouraging people. If someone were absent from Mass for a couple of weeks, people would check on them. Now, so many have left our parish no one knows who is where. (female, 49)

What has attracted me in the past is a sense of community. I still feel a sense of community and inclusion through my local parish, when I do attend, and through my parents' attendance. However, I do feel somewhat isolated, as there are no other single people attending; it is all families of varying ages. (female, 37)

When I grew up in a lovely Catholic community, it was the feeling of wonderful inclusivity—everyone was welcome. Everything was gentle, even attitudes toward homosexuals—things were more unspoken—and accepting/welcoming to all. Now there seems to be this pervasive fundamentalist element that excludes so many. (female, 37)

For a few, a genuine appreciation of parish community was nonetheless diminished by aging and/or declining congregations.

Community aspect is good. But then, few people my age attend anyway, so it's great if I feel the need to have a community of people who, on average, are at least twice my age, if not three times that. (male, 18)

The church is good at bringing communities together, but it must be said that over the years, there has been a significant decrease in the number of churchgoers since I have lived in the diocese. (male, 24)

There is a wonderful community spirit with the church regulars, however, they are an ageing population and there are not many new parishioners to take their place. (female, 47)

Others, although they recognized a sense of community as something positive, felt it was not for them.

I like that the sense of community brings people joy and support, however, any community groups can do this. (female, 28)

Community is a friendly place to belong. I believe it is nice for people to have a set of values to share and celebrate. Personally, I just do not follow those beliefs. (male, 23)

THE MASS

For many respondents, Mass retains many positive associations. *Comforting* was a word often used:

> The ritual of the Mass is wonderful, akin to being wrapped in a comfy, familiar blanket. (female, 53)
>
> I enjoy the ritual of Mass and the tradition. I like the fact that it is the same wherever I go. (female, 51)
>
> The Mass will always be a comfort and, no matter where I am, it feels like coming home when I go to Mass. It breaks my heart not to be able to participate fully now, that is, receiving Communion. (female, 38)
>
> The routine of Mass, while it can intimidate and isolate you at first, becomes comforting later. (female, 54)
>
> I like the feeling of comfort I get with a ritual I had taken part in my whole life. (female, 46)
>
> I love the rituals, so it makes me calm knowing that in the Church nothing changes. (female, 33)
>
> Mass feels so familiar and like coming home. (female, 53)

For some respondents, it was specifically the solemnity and reverence of the Mass that they felt had enduring value.

> I find the liturgy, particularly when conducted solemnly, very attractive, and I miss it. (male, 53)
>
> I enjoy the reverence and depth of worship at Mass. (female, 53)

I like the strictness and discipline of the Tridentine Mass. (male, 24)

For others, attending Mass, or even simply being in a church building, was valued as a place where they could encounter God.

I feel God's presence as I enter the church and appreciate the stillness/peace before Mass. I appreciate the simplicity and order of the Mass, the homily (when given) because of its directness and short message. At the early morning Mass where few people attend, I appreciate that I do not feel I am being judged....I appreciate the feeling of belonging, and only wish I could attend more frequently during the week. (male, 60)

I like the opportunity to have silence to reflect. I find some aspects of that in Taizé and devotional settings. Sadly, the cycle of prayer and silence is missing from most of parish life. There aren't the periods of daily prayer that the Church of England offers in their parishes, for example, or that is performed by monastics. I understand this is because of the focus on the Mass but, especially midweek, a short prayer service or something as an alternative may be a good option. (male, 23)

An empty church to me is a place of calm and a source of strength. (female, 33)

I like the smell of incense, the air of peace and calm, and the stained glass windows are amazing. They are relaxing, an "oasis of calm." (male, 39)

HISTORY, CULTURE, AND TRADITION

For a broad range of participants, the Catholic Church's historical longevity and significance are impressive. So, too, are

Catholicism's rich traditions of liturgical, devotional, and spiritual life, along with its wider cultural patrimony, especially its art, architecture, and music: proof, perhaps, of the enduring attraction of the *via pulchritudinis* or "way of beauty" (see Pontifical Council for Culture 2006). Many respondents also singled out the saints, in several cases by name.

The Catholic Church has been a major cultural force in European history. It has, at times, supplied a necessary spiritual discipline. I respect it for that. (male, 64)

I am attracted by the history of the Church, our roots in the Middle East, our diversity in the world, fine arts, and music. (male, 21)

The Church has a fine artistic and liturgical tradition (male, 27)

I like its strong identity, authenticity, holiness, its historicity, continuity, being for saints and sinners, aesthetics, clarity and rationality of teachings (in most cases), and the combination of scripture and tradition. (female, 51)

I love Catholic theology, liturgy, devotion, art, and music. (female, 19)

Much of the great music and art was brought about by the patronage of the Church. (female, 74)

I am attracted to the Mass, the liturgy, prayer, meditation, monasticism...the various spiritualities—Benedictine, Franciscan, Ignatian, etc., and their embodiment in the congregations which have developed from them. (male, 76)

I like the rosary, Mary, female saints and religious, pilgrimages, and art. (female, 18)

I like the way the Catholic Church feels familiar, maybe it is the smell of the incense and candles....I also like the fact that the Catholic Church is not afraid to use art, visual imagery, sculpture, and decoration to adorn the building inside and out. (female, 61)

I enjoy the architecture of old churches and cathedrals, the music and incense. (male, 59)

There is a magic about the church, at times, like Christmas and Easter. You can't describe it. I loved the choir at Westminster Cathedral at my brother's diaconal ordination, and the architecture of some churches. It's an English landscape; it's beautiful. It helps define the English landscape and cityscape in a positive way. (male, 37)

One respondent noted that he valued the Church's "universality" (male, 52). This point was echoed in the comments of others:

I like the global tradition. You can attend Mass in America or Africa, for example, and you are spiritually uplifted. (male, 36)

The fact that it can be found throughout the world is a comforting thought, despite my misgivings about certain doctrines. (female, 68)

Linked to this, one respondent commented that she valued the use of Latin in the Church:

Its rich culture of sacred music and art (which we rarely ever get to experience during Mass). The use of Latin—it is strange that all other main religions have a single language that unites beyond the vernacular, but ours seems to be being taken away from us, leaving us divided and impoverished. The beauty of the Latin rite is that even if travelling you can communicate in prayer with people from all diverse cultures and countries. This is less and less possible with the Latin language not being passed on. (female, 33)

CHARITABLE OUTREACH

The charitable work of the Church and its members is a recurrent theme. As one sixty-nine-year-old man commented, "The Church does an enormous amount of good."

> I admire the fact that the Catholic Church is the biggest provider of health and education after governments in the world. (female, 64)
>
> It has soft power. Its reach is virtually ubiquitous, and I believe this could be important in several ways, such as monitoring modern slavery, for example. It also contributes greatly to education and health worldwide. And it's good for charity. (female, 79)
>
> I love the idea that throughout the world, the Catholic Church is strongly involved in helping the poor and needy. (female, 54)
>
> Impressive is the work of Catholic charities in delivering Christ's message of love to all people regardless of faith. If we read/take the gospel seriously, we should be the most revolutionary body on earth! With 1.2 billion members, imagine how much good we could bring to the world! (male, 67)
>
> I admire the work of organizations like CAFOD. There are many selfless individuals who work hard all their lives in the service of others—many are Catholics. Many help in food banks. (female, 75)

Many also recognized the selflessness of individuals in the Church.

> What still attracts me to the church is the generosity and care shown by some Catholics to others less fortunate. (male, 60)
>
> There are good people doing good things to help their fellow man and they channel it through the Church, and many are good to know. By their deeds shall you know them. (male, 68)

Movingly, one forty-two-year-old woman commented, "The Catholic Church could heal the world."

POPE FRANCIS

There has been much talk of a perceived, or hoped for, "Pope Francis effect" upon people's perceptions of Catholicism, and as a means of drawing people (back) to the Church. While such impressions are notoriously hard to quantify (see Schmitz 2016), he certainly seems to have struck a chord with some of our respondents. When asked what still attracted them to the Church, one fifty-eight-year-old man simply answered, "Pope Francis." He was also featured in the responses of several others:

Pope Francis is inspirational, and I am so glad that he is addressing issues of social justice and taking the planet into account as well as the people. (female, 42)

The new open, sympathetic, and merciful approach of Pope Francis, and his emphasis on poverty through his way of life and attitude. (male, 67)

Pope Francis is a real hope for the future and a humble man whose words reach all. (female, 45)

Some focused on what they saw as the reform measures in the Church that are being introduced by Pope Francis. Often, the pope was cited as a contrast to things in the Church they disliked.

The present Pope is a great asset and is trying to return the Church to its roots in Christ. (female, 79)

Things are changing with the new pope. The Church is starting to be less authoritarian and more communal. (female, 40)

The most attractive thing is Pope Francis being a bit of a "leftie" and a man choosing to live simply, while trying to reform the corrupt side of the Vatican. (female, 64)

In some cases, the (perceived) opposition between the pope and the Church was taken to an extreme. For example, one sixty-year-old man responded, "I do not recognize the gospel in the current institutional Church, apart from Francis, Bishop of Rome."

OTHER FACTORS

There was a sharp divide between those respondents who, despite everything, still pledged their affiliation to the Catholic Church as "the *one true Church!*" (female, 73), and those who felt that the Catholic Church had strayed from and distorted Christ's original teachings. In the former group, respondents said they loved the Church when it upheld Catholic teachings; in the latter group, respondents said that they loved the message of Christ, which they felt was not expressed in magisterial teaching or pastoral practice. Let's first consider the comments of the former group:

It is the one true Church from Peter, the rock upon whom Jesus built his Church and [to whom he] handed the keys to the kingdom. It maintains all the sacraments. The pope is great, as were the others over my past fifty or so years. (male, 52)

When it is orthodox and adheres to the teachings of Christ and fulfills its role in being countercultural, that is, anti-abortion, anti-homosexual marriage....I love the Catholic Church. (male, 56)

The teaching of the Church is sound and not superficial as some new gatherings. (male, 63)

The Catholic Church holds fast to what it believes, even if this is not popular. (female, 57)

A number cited their appreciation for the Church's moral teaching—"A strong line on what is right and wrong" (male, 62)—specifically, along with its values for the raising of children.

It helps bring up people into a good routine and instill good morals. (female, 28)

It offers good grounding and values for children growing up, which continue into adulthood. (male, 49)

It provides the values on how to be a good person and how to make the world a better place. (male, 37)

It is a good moral compass for adults and children alike. Very good to share a faith with other members of the community. (male, 41)

It is a place I go when the material world gets too much, and I need reminding that there are more important things in life. (female, 33)

Relatedly, one seventy-one-year-old respondent said that what she loved about the Catholic Church was, "the comfort of certainty. I miss that." For another, it was "the love of Our Lord. That's the attractive part" (male, 50).

For others, while they expressed admiration for the person and message of Christ, they felt that the teaching and practice of the Church was in opposition to this:

The gospel message should *always take precedence* over Canon Law, tradition, conservative attitudes generally. (male, 60)

What attracts me is what Jesus said, as recorded in the Gospels. (male, 35)

The Church tries to follow the teachings of Jesus Christ who I still hold to be one of the greatest beings to walk this earth. Such a shame his teachings have been distorted by those seeking to manipulate for their own personal gain/power! Why all the pomp and ceremony though? Do you really think Jesus would approve? (male, 32)

In chapter 1, we referred to some of the negative experiences respondents had had with clergy. However, there were also those who singled out their parish priests—past and present—as what still attracted them to the Catholic Church:

A good priest can be wonderful, a support to parishioners and can invigorate faith. (female, 45)

I am proud to be a cradle Catholic—and I love the Church—my local church in [X] is beautiful and our [parish priest] is wonderful. The parish Sister, formerly an old teacher of mine, was invaluable to my family while my mother was terminally ill at home. (female, 48)

As it is my birth religion, it is part of my life, and I have found comfort at difficult times, but much of this is due to the priest at the time and his grasp of the struggles of the day-to-day life of his parishioners. (female, 62)

We have a new priest at our church in [X], and his way of preaching is fantastic. He is engaging, relevant, and inspiring. (male, 31)

There are some very nice priests. Fr. [X], for example, is a wonderful man; a true Christian. If only others would follow his example. (male, 78)

In my church, the priest, although old fashioned, is welcoming and funny. (female, 38)

I like the down-to-earth and genuinely lovely nature of my parish priest. (male, 27)

Meanwhile, others recognize how the Church has impacted others for the best, even if they feel it is not, or no longer, for them:

My nan and mum are very much of the Catholic faith and are very good people. It makes them happy. (female, 30)

I am only really attracted to the Church when I hear individuals' stories of their own faith, and how important it is for them. (female, 21)

It's made my brother [a transitional deacon] happy. (male, 30)

CONCLUSION

Our findings suggest that, despite distancing themselves from the Church, many respondents still found much about the Catholic Church attractive. The sense of community was popular among respondents, who frequently commented on the attractiveness of "community spirit," inclusiveness (all ages and nationalities), "feeling at home," the church community as an extension of the family, the welcome, and the "selflessness" of many individuals within it. Many also spoke of the ritual of the Mass, the solemnity and depth of the liturgy, and a persisting appreciation of the

Church's sacraments, devotions (especially the Rosary), and saints. A number commented on the feeling of peace and calm when they walked into an empty church. A considerable number of comments were received on the cultural heritage of the Church—its holiness and continuity—and its adherence to moral values, which for those with children was important in enabling children to know the difference between right and wrong. Some also commented on the charitable outreach of the Church across the world, particularly as the "biggest provider of health care and education after governments," and those who mentioned Pope Francis often also spoke of his witness within this general theme.

That those who have stopped attending Mass or distanced themselves from the Church still find some things attractive is very positive. In the following chapter, we will explore their views on what, if anything, they feel could or would bring them back to the Church.

4

WHAT MIGHT BRING THEM BACK?

L ater in the survey, all respondents were asked, "Can you imagine yourself returning to the Church? If so, what specific things might the Church do to help toward this?" A sizable number indicated that they could not—or, as in some cases, "absolutely not" or "never"—consider returning to Church. For a minority of these, such finality was accompanied by a palpable sense of sorrow: "No—too damaged—so sad" (female, 49), as one person stated. Others feared that, despite wanting to return, they would not be welcomed:

> I am Catholic in my heart and sometimes feel angry and upset that I no longer feel welcome within the Catholic Church. My ex-husband made me have an abortion and I then divorced him, so with those two crosses against my name, I don't feel that I can now step inside a Catholic Church. Although I have now met a wonderful man, whom I will marry, and am extremely upset to know that I won't be able to be married in my faith. (female, 43)

For a slight majority of respondents, the issue was not quite so closed. At the cooler end, some respondents expressed significant skepticism that it would happen; and then, *only if* certain major changes were to take place either in their own lives or (more often) in the Church. Among the latter, major changes to, or the repeal of, clear magisterial teachings—"it would take...a sea-change in doctrine" (male, 27); "radically rethinking its doctrine on so many issues" (female, 50); "rethink teachings I don't agree with" (female, 47)—were often set as "conditions." Much warmer, and more realistic, were the significant numbers who clearly hoped, or indeed fully expected to return. For many such people, the Catholic Church was, despite everything, still in some sense "home":

> After being estranged for many years, entering a Catholic Church still gives me a feeling of warmth and comfort. At these times I feel the pull of identity. (female, 49)
>
> There is not really anything stopping me from returning. I just need encouragement and to reconnect with my faith. (male, 64)
>
> It may seem contradictory, but I don't really feel as though I have left! I tell people that perhaps I have taken a detour and may one day find myself back on the main road! (female, 68)
>
> I can see it happening, but not yet. (female, 51)

Other respondents commented that circumstances in their personal lives meant they currently had no time to attend Mass. However, they could either foresee, or indeed actively looked forward to, a time when things might be different:

> Admittedly, these days—working full time, with kids, own interests, and own friends—I do not feel a need to attend church as I do not get out of it as much as when I meet up with some good friends....I only have two days in the week (Saturday and Sunday) to fit in everything, and therefore, this is not the right time for me now. Maybe when I retire, I will feel a need to reconnect, but at this moment in time, I do not, I am afraid. (female, 52)
>
> I would like to attend every week with my sons, but life seems to get in the way! (female, 45)
>
> Yes, I would love to attend Mass, but having to work weekends and shifts puts me at a disadvantage. (female, 45)

My current nonattendance is mostly due to physical circumstances, so when my health is better I may have the energy to attend church. (female, 37)

Some felt that any change that would need to take place first would be their own rather than something the Church could or should do:

If I returned to the Church, it would be a result of a personal change of heart, not a change in the actions of the Church. (female, 19)

It's not the Church that needs to do something, it's me. (female, 49)

The Church wouldn't have to do anything. It would have to come from me. I know what the Church is about, so there's not much more the Church can do. (male, 30)

Our primary aim, here, is to convey the answers of our participants: recording a person's comment does not, of course, imply endorsement. Here again, we will structure the main, recurrent themes under a discrete set of subheadings. These include the following:

1. The Hard to Reach

2. Rethinking Community

3. Church Teaching

4. Changes in Practice, Attitudes, Image

5. The Liturgy

6. "Accept Me as I Am"

7. Coming Home

THE HARD TO REACH

In recent years, American books and articles on people leaving the Church—of which there are now a great many—have started to speak of a group referred to as "dones" (e.g., Packard and Hope 2015). In basic terms, these "are people who are disillusioned with church. Though they were committed to the church for years...they no longer attend. Whether because they're dissatisfied with the structure, social message, or politics of the institutional church, they've decided they are better off without organized religion" (Packard 2015). While the term was coined to refer to American Evangelicals, there are clear analogues within our British Catholic sample.

While the true focus of this chapter is the *why they might return*, we would be doing our respondents a disservice if we did not first give due attention to those who, for various reasons, said that they either could not or would not, or, at least, that they could not imagine ever doing so. In terms of evangelistic or pastoral outreach, such people are, to put it mildly, "hard to reach."

Among these "Catholic dones," we include those who expressed an active desire *not* ever to return. For some, this was combined with a feeling of relief or liberation in having left in the first place.

It would feel like being chained again to a doctrine of rules and regulations that disempower you to be free to worship God in Spirit and Truth. (female, 53)

It's clear the Church will not ever be a good place for me. (male, 32)

I feel fortunate to have the time to properly disentangle myself and understand that my quality of life and thought are richer without the Church. (male, 42)

Maybe, if there would have been more input by the Church when I was younger, the situation would be reversed. But it's too late now. (female, 42)

No, I would not start practicing again. For what? If the Church woke up and dealt with issues, then possibly. It only cares now because pews are empty, money is tight, parishes are closing, and priests are retiring. Yes, I'm cynical. I've been around awhile. They didn't listen years and years ago, and now it suits them. Surprise, surprise. (female, 64)

Sadly, one eighteen-year-old man expressed eager anticipation at not having to attend Mass anymore: "Forced to go once a month. Once I leave the house for university, I will not be returning."

For others, the driving influence is that, in the words of one, their "spiritual home is elsewhere now" (male, 48). One evangelical Christian said,

Why would I start practicing again? I have a community and I have the Bible. Above all, I have faith in Jesus Christ. The Catholic Church...needs to ask what it seeks. Does it really want to bring change to individual lives or does it want to stem its own decline? If things were stable, with healthy full pews, would the Church care about me and my faith? The Church, if it's serious, needs to invest in people and provide the support that will build and grow faith. Often, the homily was short and left me wondering about the faith. Hard issues were always avoided! No deep exploration of the teachings of the Church or the Bible. External changes alone won't work though, it confuses and frustrates people, and that's part of the cause of decline post-Vatican II. Rearranging chairs on a sinking ship won't change much—aside from angering the people on the top deck waiting for a life boat! Hearts and minds—relational work and conversion of heart—is what's needed. That wasn't on the survey as an option, sadly. Maybe you should come to my Church and not the other way around. ;). (male, 27)

One Baptist respondent said,

> I don't see wide signs that God is working at the parish level. If Jesus Christ isn't changing hearts and transforming people, then they start to get frustrated with rules and doctrine. To then change those things to keep them interested is a sign of a damaged and corrupted institution. One, I would say with sadness, that has lost sight of Jesus Christ. The questions I got asked here are concerning to me. If the gospel was being taught and the Catholic Church was learning from growing Churches, it would know that it can't grow and impact with its current doctrine, dogma, and values. They need a better approach. It's depressing that they don't seem to "get it" after all these years. That's why I won't come back. (female, 20)

Many others, however, no longer feel the need for any Church in their current lives.

> I believe I live to my own Christian moral standards and don't feel the need to attend church—as I often have nothing in common with many people who attend and feel uncomfortable. (female, 44)
>
> I have developed my Christianity through spirituality. I talk with God daily and have tremendous gratitude for all the help he gives me. (female, 58)
>
> I will never return to any organized religion. I am a good person; I help people; I do what I can to assist others around the world, but I don't have a religious doctrine attached to any of it. People just need to be nice to each other without the tag of "Catholic," etc. (female, 47)

Finally, some said they would not attend again, owing to their lack of faith:

I cannot imagine ever regaining my faith. There is nothing the Church can do for me, but I appreciate and respect what it does for others. (male, 29)

I will return only if my belief in God changes. (male, 37)

I can't see myself getting enough faith to take Communion again. (male, 60)

I'd attend for my family, for major feasts or holidays. But my beliefs have changed, so I can't see anything beyond that. (female, 42)

I'm not sure I believe in God any more, but that feeling also leaves me feeling lost at times! (female, 56)

RETHINKING COMMUNITY

Several respondents expressed a desire to belong to a parish community, with some people citing a hope for personal, emotional support.

I would love to go back to church, but we need more caring, empathetic priests. (female, 49)

I would like some help and support to make sense of, and manage, my father's recent death. (female, 52)

[What would help is] talking to someone about my issues one-to-one. (female, 55)

One fifty-five-year-old respondent said he would appreciate "a more friendly, welcoming, and active parish"; others had suggestions for how this might look like in practice:

If I had access to a Bible study group or some opportunity where I could talk about my faith with others and listen to their ideas, I would be so much more inspired. If I go to Mass, I go by myself, and it is a very lonely experience. People don't want to discuss faith over tea and biscuits after Mass, so when I do go, it just feels like I am going to "do the right thing." (male, 35)

I would like to see parish priests who will listen to their parishioners and work *with* them and not over them, using their skills, qualifications, and experience. I am looking for real Christian community—a 24/7 loving, caring community—not just a mainly Sunday, ritual, liturgical Church. I would like to see more Spirit-led activity, praise, and worship—like at the World Youth Days, and using the many gifts of the Holy Spirit....Many do not know how to have a personal relationship with the living Jesus and how to pray from the heart. (male, 52)

I would want to join a church where the focus wasn't entirely on the family, and where all types of people are welcome. Sometimes there is nothing worse than the assumption that, as an unmarried woman, you would be willing to take on all the tea making and washing up or organize another tabletop sale....I do know [that] when I attended [an Anglo-Catholic parish], I began to grow again. I began to love God and behave better because the created space naturally drew me toward that. I still try to live in that loving way now, although I often fail. Coming to that table every week, with all the other members of the diverse congregation, was like a glimpse of heaven....Sometimes, the Catholic Church tries too hard to control how God comes through. Please don't. Think about your spaces and communities, and let God come through. (female, 42)

I think it would help if the Church created more programs and pathways for people in parishes and dioceses that engaged and supported them to live as faithful Catholics throughout life. There needs to be more focus on nurturing married couples, young people and those in the 18 to 35 age range....Too many people feel lost, and the Church needs to challenge and up its game. Actions are louder than words. The Church, each parish, needs to be more mission-based. There's often the usual efforts to collect money or do homeless work, but there's not the more difficult dialogue around faith and family. (male, 34)

I would like to see specific groups and activities, for example, for converts, older people, youth, and so on. My current [non-Catholic] church has link groups where there are ten or fifteen of us who meet once a month and support each other and have Bible study and social time. We also use the group to volunteer and fill rotas for the church, and it stops people from feeling alone and getting overlooked, especially if sick or struggling. (female, 65)

One thirty-one-year-old man, who described himself as a Christian of no denomination, said, "Promote community; offer a Mass with modern music; invite guest speakers; hear more about what faith is like today in the real world; provide something for the children." While one thirty-year-old woman wanted "more social things after Mass for people in their 30s," another young woman (twenty) said the Church should become "more accessible for young people": "I don't want it to be crazy, I like the peace you feel when you go into a church. I'm looking for something more interesting, meaningful, and easy to understand." Still another respondent said,

There needs to be a focus on young people and building them up in various ways. I was mostly left to my own devices, aside from sitting through Mass for an hour a week. I don't think most people can stay involved if that's all there is as a connection. (male, 28)

A fifty-three-year old woman now attending a Holy Trinity Brompton plant church felt that families need to receive more understanding: "Become more flexible and understanding of the emotional and financial pressures that families are under these days and less condemnatory when people get things wrong, stressing the 'forgiving Father' heart of God." A thirty-seven-year-old woman said, "There needs to be a more sensible experience for children....Friendliness is so simple, but my parish has been so unwelcoming to my children and me."

CHURCH TEACHING

Not surprisingly, given the attention doctrinal issues have received earlier in this book (primarily in chapter 2, though interweaved throughout), around a quarter of respondents said that, for them to consider returning to the Catholic Church, teachings in certain areas would need to be changed. As already observed, specific suggestions were varied, and the desired nature of doctrinal change was not uniform among respondents. While most favored greater congruence between Church teaching and modern liberal norms, a notable minority urged the Church to hold firm to traditional positions already clearly articulated by the Magisterium.

Regarding the former group, one respondent suggested, "Modernize" (female, 52); another stated, "Change out-of-date doctrines" (male, 43). These were sentiments echoed in many other responses, often as part of a wider list of *desiderata*. One forty-one-year-old commented that she would not return to the church "unless there are some pretty massive changes, such as owning up to the history of child sexual abuse, acceptance of marriage equality, women leaders, and for the leadership to be leaders on issues of global importance." Others made the following comments:

There should be less focus on God and more on what people can do to help each other and how to live a good life. (male, 18)

The Church needs to treat all humans as equals. It needs to openly admit that a group of men cherry-picked the books and verses it wished to include in the Bible using a set of criteria to fit their agenda and that other works were barred just because they did not fit the agenda. (female, 43)

While the Catholic Church does not actively accept gay marriage, I cannot view it as a positive place. Discrimination is not acceptable on any level. (female, 28)

If the Church modernized and became less black and white about its teaching, including the requirement to attend church every Sunday, I would feel more inclined to attend more regularly. (female, 51)

I would consider returning to the Church if it became more inclusive of people who are LGBT. (female, 31)

Many expressed the changes they desired in terms of "following Pope Francis" (female, 61):

Pope Francis and his liberal views make me feel more comfortable with my faith, as he is much more forgiving and is tackling corruption within the Church. I think more of this needs to happen before I would return to church. (female, 27)

I am delighted that Pope Francis wants to smell of the sheep and does not live in pomp and splendor. Once the "Francis effect" filters down far enough here in the United Kingdom, I may feel able to return to the Church, as it will truly be a Church of and for the people of God, not just the Church of the anointed and appointed few. He is upsetting the career cronies decorated in lace climbing up the greasy poles in the Vatican. I do hope they will "see the light" and realize that the Church should be about the reality of life as it is lived, especially by those who are poor, marginalized, disenfranchised, and sidelined. The Church should not be about power, money, dressing up in finery, self-satisfaction, and arrogance. (female, 53)

In one sense, I haven't left the Church. If the directions taken by Pope Francis continue, and his approach finds its way through to the wider Church, then like many others I will be willing to become active again. (male, 76)

Some respondents expressed their desire for change in Church teachings, but did not hold out much hope:

Reform may take many years to take hold—and I have only one life to live, so I have taken it elsewhere. (female, 55)

Given that roughly one-tenth of respondents gave the lack of recognition of their remarriage as a reason for their leaving the Church, it is unsurprising that some called for the remarried to be able to receive holy communion. One respondent, whose frustrations in this area have been quoted previously, called for the annulment process to be "made easier" (female, 47).[1] Others responses include:

A change in the policy of allowing divorced and remarried Catholics to receive Communion would help, but I'd also need to see a more liberal approach to other excluded people as well. (male, 53)

I would not return unless the Church changes its mind on marrying divorced people and accepting them rather than treating them as outcasts. (female, 35)

In contrast, as noted earlier, other respondents noted emphatically that the Church's teachings should *not* be changed—unless, perhaps, they were changed to what they had been in the past:

---

1. Please note: The survey was done in the months immediately following the Vatican's announcement of changes—often characterized in media reports as "streamlining," or "making easier"—to the annulment process in September 2015. It is not clear if the respondent here was referring to this or not.

I would never return if the Church gives way to this craze for "modernity" and submits to altering its doctrine(s) to suit the "spirit of the age" (as if that itself didn't change regularly!), which is weasel-speak for "telling people that whatever they want to do is OK." The devil must be laughing his head off. (female, 73)

I consider returning whenever I find a Catholic church that practices Catholicism properly rather than ignoring and disregarding ordinary people and insisting on liberalization at the expense of the faith. For a Catholic, the way to freedom for all (equality for women, inclusion of migrants, and welcoming the poor) is in Catholic teaching. Hence, what we need is better education in doctrine and traditions, not simply jettisoning traditions to bow to the demands of liberal capitalism. The Catholic Church needs to listen to its people while also keeping true to its teaching. So many Catholic priests seem to have lost their faith. They need to renew their faith rather than keep apologizing for it. (female, 33)

CHANGES IN PRACTICE, ATTITUDES, AND IMAGE

Alongside changes in doctrine, many respondents called for changes in the way the Church lives out her mission in the world. This echoes a sentiment expressed earlier about the seeming divergence between Jesus's message and the Church's way of living it out. For example, one respondent wrote,

Ask the question, "What would Jesus do?" to make the Catholic Church better. Do you really believe the Catholic Church is the best representation of Christ's values? A humble man from humble beginnings with a message of peace, love, nonmaterialism. No one would say the Catholic Church is humble or not materialistic. (male, 32)

Some emphasized the need for perceived practices and attitudes to change, while others emphasized the work that needs to be done on the Church's image in the world. One twenty-three-year-old man, for instance, said that being Catholic was now "a toxic brand." This image was reflected in the opinions of others:

> There'd have to be drastic changes in the Church for me to return, including giving back all the gold and jewels you have stashed in churches and in the Vatican to the impoverished, dying poor, rather than just slapping them in the face with a Bible. (male, 26)

> The Church needs to reach out to the community, recognize modern-day diversity, and not appear to be an exclusive club. (male, 63)

> The whole ethos needs to change. Elderly men should not have an overwhelming charge of decision-making. (female, 68)

> The Catholic Church really needs to change and become less of a Catholic club before I could even consider returning. With the reaction to Islam, there seems to be a slight tendency to move backwards and become more rigorous. (female, 68)

> Keep it simple and compassion/love-filled in word, deed, and teaching. Look to the ancient/Celtic monastic ways of simple living, grounded in clear morals, but show compassion for others. Strip away the man-made add-ons and dictatorial "must-dos" that no longer reflect us. Move away from a patriarchal approach and be welcoming and inclusive. (female, 41)

> I would consider returning if the Church admitted mistakes or addressed its problems that occurred in the last fifty years. I'm not against working with a culture. But the Church does not seem to know what it's doing. It will, I fear, fall into factions like the Anglicans and break off to serve its own conferences. (female, 64)

The Church needs to stop playing catch up and media/political influence games....It just brings scorn and makes being Catholic a toxic brand. Muslims don't get caught up in all the media fighting with cultural change, and so on, and they aren't doing so bad in converts/attrition. (male, 23)

Currently, the system seems too hierarchical and, due to many scandals that have emerged, this hierarchy seems untrustworthy. To resolve this, I would want to see the very high priests become more personable and available to their community (at the moment, it is like a corporate business, where the "executives" are rarely seen, though orders seem to emerge from their assistants). (female, 21)

The Church leaders need to be less arrogant and self-serving. There needs to be less people at the top telling others what to do. Sometimes there appears to be more emphasis on operating procedures than [living] the gospel. (male, 45)

I would become more active in the Church if it were to reach out more to the poor and members of other faiths, so we can include Muslims, atheists, and others in our family. (male, 21)

THE LITURGY

The centrality of the Mass to Catholic life and identity, also noted in earlier chapters, emerges in the context of this chapter. Accordingly, since liturgical dissatisfaction was often cited as a reason for people leaving, it is no surprise to see changes, or the undoing of changes, to the liturgy featured heavily here. Before outlining these, and further underscoring the significance of this area, let us consider the comments regarding the realities of what a return to Mass might entail for them.

I have a fear of attending Sunday Mass because it reminds me of my past [relationships] and what subsequently happened [i.e., adultery, followed by divorce and remarriage]. I fear what people might think and believe! I fear the awkwardness of not receiving Holy Communion—having to remain in the pew attracts the attention of others (possibly magnified by my imagination) and creates a distance between myself and God. (male, 60)

I can't imagine returning to Mass right now. I might attend Mass more often if I did not feel that I was being hypocritical. I guess I could simply not say or sing parts of the Mass which I cannot believe in, but regardless, I would feel by my presence that I am "pretending" to believe in things that are being sung in the hymns or said on my behalf by the priest. It is therefore difficult to see what could be done. (male, 54)

It would be very helpful if there was a detailed program/printed structure of the Mass—when to stand up, when to kneel, what the priest will say and how the congregation is to respond. (female, 33)

More concretely, a few respondents were clear that a "simple" or "quiet" Mass would bring them back:

If the Church had a simple Mass with the basics for mainstream returners without heavy Catholicism, yes, I would consider it. (female, 68)

I would not consider returning to the Church while the current priest is in our parish and with the production—all-singing, all-dancing Masses—he puts on. Mass should be toned down and simple with at least one Sunday Mass where prayers are not sung but spoken. (female, 50)

In contrast, others responded that they would consider returning if the Mass were livelier:

> Changing the Mass and being more relevant would help me return to Church. The priests need to be more engaging instead of being—but not in all cases—monotone. (female, 47)
>
> Allow the Mass to become something different and more inspiring. Allow the format of the Mass to change. (male, 41)
>
> Offer an "express Mass" of half an hour with cheerful singing. (female, 43)
>
> The sermon should be a genuine commentary on life today based on the daily readings. Use modern interpretations of the Bible. We know so much more now about the context of the writings. The Catholic Church should foster community service, not proselytizing. In our specific parish, there should be a meeting space at the entrance to the church so that people can gather after Mass. Less emphasis on formal liturgy but a more varied church service. What is the rationale for the same structure of the Mass all the time? And for the priest reading the words? (female, 63)

In direct contrast to both, other respondents asserted—and in no uncertain terms—that wider provision of a more traditional and solemn liturgy would help to entice people back:

> Drop the Children's Liturgy, have a less hippy Mass with no talking in church. Clear teaching about the Eucharist. Stop the hippy 1970s-style Mass. There are too many ministers of the Eucharist. At one Mass there were also 37 altar servers, of which 32 were girls. Need to stop ordinary people blessing people at Communion. The priest's job is pointless. (male, 24)

Go back to the practice of the old Mass and ditch Vatican II. Didn't Pope Paul VI say that the smoke of Satan had entered the Vatican? (male, 56)

I would consider returning if the respect comes back and people realize that this is the house of the Lord and it is precious. Children should be brought up with this respect ingrained in them. (female, 73)

To turn now to more prosaic matters, one woman commented that practical changes should be made to make Mass easier for young families to attend and stated that a family Mass that lasted one-and-a-half hours was too long for small children. Others made the following observations:

The building is very family unfriendly—impossible to get buggies in, no place to take crying children except out in the cold/rain so that you, yourself, miss out on Mass. (female, 32)

Why call something a "Children's Liturgy" if it is just the same Mass as normal. Is it just a way to warn those that don't like children in church to stay away from that specific Mass?! (female, 33)

Having given thought to what a return to the Church would entail, a few respondents mentioned confession—both as a potential stumbling block and in the context of what would help them to receive this sacrament:

I would love to return to the Church, but I could never go to Confession. (female, 67)

By the way, please don't do face-to-face confessions, unless requested by individuals—it's really embarrassing and a stumbling block to returnees. (female, 51)

Absolutely, I would like to return, but I will need to attend Reconciliation during the Year of Mercy to be forgiven, hopefully, for not only recent sins but a terrible sin I committed many years ago—a medical termination that I have never confessed to due to shame and fear. (female, 48)

If I returned, I would dread trying to recount 55 years of sin in Confession! (female, 71)

"ACCEPT ME AS I AM"

While many respondents referred to certain teachings they did not agree with, a few expressed their personal sadness at not feeling accepted *in themselves* by the Church. One forty-two-year-old woman expressed her view that the Church needed to accept people as "complex" human beings:

I would need to be a hybrid person, a person whose identity is complex, a sinner who is on a journey toward God—and to fully inhabit that identity and to be able to talk about it. I would like to feel welcomed as an imperfect being....A place where serious discussions can be held and it's OK to explore things deeply; where you can talk about doubts and difficulties, embrace complexity, and go forward in a positive way.

A few respondents, who described themselves as gay, expressed their experience of not feeling accepted by the Church:

I would love to feel welcomed for who I am, for the Church to change her teaching on homosexuality and make us welcome and accepted members. (female, 53)

Stop treating me like a demon! (male, 50)

A big barrier to returning is the specific issue of feeling accepted, not needing to hide my sexuality, or being treated as a second-class citizen and as a sinner who is only there on sufferance. (female, 51)

Others who were either divorced and remarried or cohabiting expressed similar views:

I don't expect approval of my lifestyle since my divorce and the fact that I have a new partner, but I would appreciate a little understanding and recognition that I still have faith and something to offer. (female, 38)

Accept divorcées, allow them to marry in church, and accept those who have done things which are against traditional Catholic values. I want to be part of the Church again. (female, 43)

I live with a partner, and we have children. I would like to marry, but my partner would not agree to attend the church or courses regularly, therefore, I feel I will forever be condemned as a sinner, because I am torn between the teachings of the Church and my love for my partner. If the Church accepted nonbelievers and was not judgmental, I might be able to convince my partner to get married in the Church. (female, 33)

Accept my family and me for who we are: sinners who need forgiveness. (male, 69)

One thirty-eight-year-old mother, who had given up attending Mass with her young daughter, said, "I would like my daughter to be made welcome. Children do make a noise, but they should be welcomed and not hushed and frowned at."

COMING HOME

Encouragingly, there were small numbers of respondents who had either recently started practicing their faith again or were seriously considering it. One forty-five-year-old man answered, "Yes, I so want to return to the Church." First, we turn to those who said that they were considering returning to Mass.

> Due to changes in circumstances, I am prepared to give it another go. (male, 56)
>
> Yes, I would really like to be involved with the Church. Possibly more mid-week Masses but to be honest, I need to prioritize better. I would also like to volunteer in the community, but do not know how to progress this. (female, 45)
>
> Yes, I would like to return. I keep a watchful distance. I go occasionally and love to sing—maybe I could go back for a music group. (female, 54)
>
> I am still a Catholic. I only go when I feel led by the Holy Spirit. I decided to stop for a while and need to build up more confidence to return. I started feeling the same feelings, but I do not want to give up. (female, 40)
>
> I intend returning. I will go back just for my own peace of mind. I won't judge anyone else or expect anything other than my own sense of returning to Jesus. I may visit my church in the quiet of the week rather than at Mass. (female, 51)

For at least one participant, our survey seems to have been a welcome sign pointing to an eventual return:

> Of course, I will return to church and Mass when I am ready, and strangely during the past few weeks, I have been thinking of returning to Mass regularly. I know it will happen when God sets the right time. I saw this survey and wanted very much to take part. Many thanks Bishop Philip for the opportunity to do so. (female, 65)

Others said they might consider going in the future for the sake of their children:

> If I have children, I would want them brought up with this religion. (female, 26)
>
> Perhaps when I have a family of my own. (female, 35)
>
> I would like my children, in the future, to have Christian values and would probably have them baptized too due to the family tradition. (male, 23)
>
> I see real value in raising a family in the context of the Catholic Church, and so when my priorities are focused on starting a family, I will reconsider. (female, 25)
>
> I feel responsible [for] my young children...and for that reason I wish to return...but now, I'm going through a tough time. (female, 41)
>
> My boy will be taking his First Communion, so we will return then. (male, 49)
>
> My son is starting to attend the church because he has just started reception in a Catholic school and we talk about it at home...

praying, talking about Jesus, and so on. I might go with him at some point, but I am still hurt by the way I was treated [when a priest refused to baptize my son]. (female, 33)

I feel that I am not being a good role model for my children. I would like to improve this. (female, 46)

Others shared that they had been going to Mass in recent weeks. They all expressed certain hesitations about their experience so far:

I have recently returned, encouraged by this Pope and a Latin Mass. Usually, the English Mass is noisy, sloppily performed, without dignity, and lacks all sense of the numinous and opportunity for silent prayer. The hymns are usually banal in the extreme. (male, 71)

I came back to the Catholic Church having been away for 43 years. Do I believe? I honestly don't know. I do believe that we should love others as ourselves, and that love is stronger than hate....My reasons for returning are numerous: (1) Gratitude for something fantastic that happened in my life after I prayed; (2) a desire for my daughter to have a sense of "community"; (3) a hope that she will be "protected" from the evil in the world; (4) a desire for her to learn good "moral standards" and to grow up being kind to others; and (5) a desire for her not to feel alone in this world. However, I do feel cynical about this word "community." Does "community" really exist, or are we just a bunch of people who live near each other and scurry away like rats after the Mass is finished, not ever even speaking or knowing each other? (female, 61)

I have returned to the Church. I attend Mass, but I do struggle with the almost superior air of priests, as if they have all the answers but cannot give a reasonable answer when asked why. (female, 53)

·CONCLUSION

Our findings show that although a relatively substantial pro-portion of respondents stated that they could not see themselves coming back or would never come back, many stated that they would come back if things were different. Roughly one quarter of the respondents felt alienated through their life circumstances, mainly remarriage after divorce or issues relating to homosexual-ity. They stated that returning to the Church would be difficult because they would not feel welcome, they would feel awkward about being there, or they could not receive communion. Some felt a slight awkwardness in coming back after so long; they wanted printed sheets detailing the responses of the Mass and indicators of when to sit/kneel/stand. Others felt they needed more per-sonal encouragement—perhaps from a priest or close friend—to start attending Mass again. For some, the thought of "going to confession" caused anxiety. Overall, responses were in line with reasons given for having distanced themselves from the Church in the first place and/or what they still found attractive about the Church. Interestingly, a number commented on the appeal of more conservative practices: homilies that addressed the "hard" issues, a clear stance on traditional Christian moral positions. One respondent, who had become a Baptist, mentioned the impor-tance of changing "hearts and minds" for "rules and doctrines" to "work."

A considerable number of respondents[2] spoke about the importance of welcoming and/or being open to children; others said they wanted to return because they felt a sense of responsibil-ity for their children and wanted them to be brought up in the Catholic faith. There was some focus on the need of nurturing and supporting people within the parish, for example, married couples and young people in their thirties. Some felt they would like to see more activities developed for different age groups, with quite a few citing the need for discussion groups to explore issues like faith "in the real world." Certainly, some of the reasons given

2. Although again, as noted previously, this is likely inflated by the demographics of our survey sample.

for what would bring respondents back to the Church are inspiring, if challenging. In the last chapter, we draw on these reasons to make some practical suggestions for how these individuals, and others like them, can be further supported and welcomed back to the Church.

5

THEOLOGICAL REFLECTIONS AND PASTORAL RECOMMENDATIONS

Our survey's findings are illuminating and, while deeply challenging, offer several pathways of hope. Although a sizable proportion of participants commented that they would never or probably never return to the Church, many expressed a desire to return if things were different. In this concluding chapter, we change gear. In the previous chapters, our focus has been on faithfully representing the voices of our myriad respondents; indeed, to share the stories that they themselves have generously shared with us. Here we offer theological and pastoral reflections on how the Catholic Church, and especially parish communities, might authentically respond to the issues raised. Central are two concerns: first, to serve non- or irregularly practicing Catholics, ideally with a view to helping them return home; and second, to seek ways to ensure that fewer baptized Catholics feel so distant from the Church—or one or more aspects of it.

First, let us discuss the significant issues raised, directly or indirectly, by our participants. We will then offer ten practical recommendations that Catholic parishes might consider implementing.

HOW TO RESPOND?

While many of the respondents expressed relief or apathy about leaving the Catholic Church, many others conveyed anguish and distress. Clergy and laypeople reading their responses will have encountered a vast panorama of human experiences; and reactions will range from empathy to horror and from sorrow to confusion at what has been recounted. We reiterate our gratitude to the 256 participants for their honest responses. In the details of their experiences, some of the most pressing questions with which we struggle as humans are raised: What is our purpose? Does God truly exist, and if so, does he care about me? Why does evil exist? Is there a natural law? How am I saved? The stories shared also ask questions of the Church, herself: How does God guide the Church? Why does he allow evil to happen in the Church? How does his providence work alongside our freedom?

In many ways, the study is like moving a rock and discovering the reality of what lies beneath. The stories are a glimpse of the interface between our secular, postmodern reality and the Church, whose mission is to proclaim the good news to those within it. They are a glimpse into both the Church's failure in her mission, but also the signs of hope about how the Church might be more effective. While there is much that can be analyzed—more than is possible in this book—there are two overarching themes to consider before turning to the practical, pastoral recommendations.

The Eclipse of God from Our Culture

Living in a Western, postmodern milieu, where God has generally been rejected, the questions listed above assault Catholics from all sides. The eclipse of God from our culture results in subjectivism and materialism that influences believers just as much as nonbelievers. It is a process of "immanentization" in the term coined by Catholic philosopher, Charles Taylor, where—because the transcendent is eclipsed—meaning and significance are sought only within an enclosed, self-sufficient, naturalistic universe (Taylor 2007). Cardinal Sarah expresses how "menacing" these threats can be for Christians:

> Western man seems to have made up his mind; he has liberated himself from God; he lives without God. The new rule is to forget heaven so that man might be fully

free and autonomous. But the death of God results in the burial of good, beauty, love, and truth; if the source no longer flows, if even that water is transformed by the mud of indifference, man collapses. Good becomes evil, beauty is ugly, love becomes the satisfaction of several primal sexual instincts, and truths are all relative. (Sarah 2015, 171)

How the fallout from the eclipse of God affects Catholics is amply demonstrated in the responses. Here we list four of the main symptoms:

The struggle to believe that God exists: Many described how they drifted, sometimes unconsciously, away from the Church; they no longer saw belief as an option or struggled to believe that God exists. The stories strongly urge the Church that, in pastoral ministry, no presumptions can be made; belief cannot be taken for granted. Opportunities for discussion, exploration, and debate are needed at parish level to demonstrate the philosophical rigor and authenticity of belief in God.

An unfulfilled search for meaning in the Church: Somewhat paradoxically, most respondents stated that their spiritual needs were not met in the Church. At some point, many respondents *were* seeking God and the spiritual life but did not find their quest fulfilled in their parishes. In some parishes, the Mass is not simply the main offering of the week but the *only* offering, and for some, without catechesis, it can be impenetrable. For instance:

If I had access to a Bible study group or some opportunity where I could talk about my faith with others and listen to their ideas I would be so much more inspired. (male, 35)

I would like to feel welcomed as an imperfect being....A place where serious discussions can be held, and it's OK to explore things deeply; where you can talk about doubts and difficulties, embrace complexity, and go forward in a positive way. (female, 42)

As the *Catechism* states, "'The sacred liturgy does not exhaust the entire activity of the Church' (*Sacrosanctum Concilium*, 9): it must be preceded by evangelization, faith and conversion. It can then produce its fruits in the lives of the faithful: new life in the Spirit, involvement in the mission of the Church, and service to her unity" (*CCC* §1072). Too often in pastoral practice, the parish offers sacraments without the accompanying evangelization and catechesis that bring conversion. Again, knowledge and understanding can too often be presumed. Several excellent resources exist to help parish communities grow in their understanding of, and confidence in, the Catholic faith. See, for example, the *Evangelium* and *Why?* courses produced by the Catholic Truth Society.

The disconnect between people's thinking and the mind of the Church around morality: It is perhaps unsurprising that morality is one of the most obvious areas of disconnection. Many responses seek a radical change on key moral and doctrinal positions. For those whose lives are touched by these issues, for instance, those living through unresolved marriage issues, such moral questions can be tortuously personal and raw. Any response to what people have written here must sensitively balance both the objective and the subjective perspectives.

From the objective perspective, the eternal and unchanging nature of natural and revealed law is inescapable. The extent to which we have lost our capacity to recognize these truths attests to the pervasive "secularization of consciousness"[1] of those within the Church as much as those outside it. It also attests to the failure of methods the Church has used to pass on the faith. These methods have failed to connect with or answer the pressing questions of certain respondents.

Faced with these realities, we might be tempted to think that better and sound faith formation is the only solution to the widening gap between Church doctrine and the increasingly secularized outlook of many Catholics. The reality is more complex. Even as

---

1. Sociologist Peter Berger uses this term to denote the reality where, as a society becomes more externally secular in its culture and symbols, a corresponding internal secularization takes place in the consciousness of individuals. He writes, "This means that the modern West has produced an increasing number of individuals who look upon the world and their own lives without the benefit of religious interpretations" ([1967] 1990, 108).

far back as 1971, the *General Catechetical Directory* warned that the renewal of catechesis is endangered by those who are "unable to understand the depth of the proposed renewal, as though the issue here were merely one of eliminating ignorance of the doctrine which must be taught. According to the thinking of those people, the remedy would be more frequent catechetical instruction" (no. 9). In fact, the *Directory* argued that the entire catechetical enterprise needs to be renewed. While this topic is far wider than can be explored here,[2] we find the kernel of an answer in Pope Benedict XVI's words, where he speaks about the impact of relativism:

> An "adult" faith is not a faith that follows the trends of fashion and the latest novelty; a mature adult faith is deeply rooted in friendship with Christ. It is this friendship that opens us up to all that is good and gives us a criterion by which to distinguish the true from the false, and deceit from truth. (Homily, *Missa pro eligendo Romano Pontifice*, April 18, 2005)

A relational approach to catechesis and pastoral ministry, emphasizing, above all, a relationship with God at its heart, corresponds to the prevailing subjective perspective of a postmodern approach to morality. Pope Francis's apostolic exhortation *Amoris Laetitia* proposes such a relational approach, offering guidelines for the pastoral accompaniment of people in difficult marital situations. Bishop Egan announced in July 2016 that the Diocese of Portsmouth would begin a period of review and development of pastoral practice around the four areas of "marriage promotion, marriage preparation, marriage care, and marriage 'repair.'"[3]

The subjective approach also has its implications for homilies, a factor that will be discussed later.

---

2. Documents such as the *General Directory for Catechesis* (1997) and *Catechesi Tradendae* (1979) expound the proper place of experience in catechesis, if it is truly to transform hearts and minds.

3. Bishop Philip Egan, "Getting Married," Pastoral Letter (July 10, 2016). Available at http://www.portsmouthdiocese.org.uk/bishop/pastoral_letters/20160710-BoP-PL-Getting-Married-A4.pdf (accessed July 23, 2017).

It is also worth noting that some saw the sacrament of reconciliation as a daunting stumbling block to their return. Many of this group included those who had distanced themselves from the Church because of their circumstances (e.g., remarriage after a divorce). A certain nervousness in approaching the confessional is, in fact, a common and perfectly natural emotion—akin, one supposes, to how the prodigal son may have felt as he dejectedly, and burdened with shame, returned home to his father's house (see Luke 15:11–32). Like the prodigal son, however, those approaching the sacrament should be aware that their return will be welcomed with compassion and, indeed, joy. In the words of Christ, "There is joy in the presence of the angels of God over one sinner who repents" (Luke 15:10).

The polarization around liturgy: The final symptom of how the eclipse of God has impacted Catholics is witnessed in the polarized views around liturgy. The vastly different standpoints and views from respondents do not need to be repeated here, but they sum up the so-called liturgy wars in the decades following Vatican II. While the liturgy is the source of unity for Catholics, sadly, it has, in practice, been the source of division, and these divisions are vivid in the responses. Certainly there is no liturgical "silver bullet" that can please everyone. Furthermore, the sheer range of preferences mentioned in our sample would be very difficult for any single parish to cater to (e.g., providing several distinct Masses on a Sunday). Equally, however, one might conclude that liturgical diversity—including personal, individual *preferences*—is a part, and perhaps even a root cause, of the problem in the first place (see Sarah 2017, building on some ideas in Ratzinger 1998). These are fundamental questions for the Church, of course, that go far beyond the specific (though hugely important) issues of lapsation and disaffiliation.

These four areas, which demonstrate the impact of secularization on Catholics—loss of belief in God, an unfulfilled spiritual search for God in the Church, a disconnect between views on morality, and the polarization around liturgy—are colossal challenges for the Church and are intensely illustrated in the answers of the respondents. Overall, they urge the Church toward a wide-reaching, pastoral paradigm shift. Given the upheaval of culture that has ravaged the West since the 1960s, we face a brutal awakening that a "business-as-usual" approach to pastoral ministry is insufficient for our own self-preservation, let alone to fulfill the command of Christ to "go therefore and make disciples of all nations" (Matt 28:19). Later, we will address what this paradigm shift might look like, but first we consider the second overarching theme that emerges from the responses.

The Mystery of Evil and Disunity in the Church

Many of the respondents referenced painful and confusing human situations—ranging from minor misunderstandings to terrible abuse—that triggered their departure from the Church. The mystery of suffering is a perennial question, but when it is caused, wittingly or unwittingly, by the Church, it seems an even greater evil. Having listened carefully to these experiences, it is important to respond with humility and thoughtfulness. As with any question about evil, "no quick answer will suffice. Only Christian faith as a whole constitutes the answer to this question: the goodness of creation, the drama of sin, and the patient love of God who comes to meet man by his covenants, the redemptive Incarnation of his Son, his gift of the Spirit, his gathering of the Church, the power of the sacraments, and his call to a blessed life to which creatures are invited to consent in advance, but from which, by a terrible mystery, they can also turn away in advance" (*CCC* §309).

While "the gathering of the Church" is intended in God's plan to be the context of salvation for the entire world, it has always been throughout history (exemplified in some of the stories we have read) a stumbling block. Of course, each story is more complex than what has been recounted, and God alone penetrates fully each situation and each human heart. But it must be a source of sorrow for the Church when any person falls away, either of their own volition or because of hurt caused by the Church.

When asked about the child abuse scandal, Pope Benedict XVI commented,

> It is a particularly serious sin when someone who is actually supposed to help people toward God, and to whom a child or a young person is entrusted in order to find the Lord, abuses him instead and leads him away from the Lord. As a result the faith as such becomes unbelievable,

and the Church can no longer present herself credibly as the herald of the Lord. (Pope Benedict XVI 2010, 25)

These words can be applied also to any situation where the Church leads a person away from the Lord, and not to him. *Lumen Gentium* (no. 48) defined the Church as the "universal sacrament of salvation." Her visible signs should lead a person to the invisible reality of communion with Christ. In the words of theologian Henri de Lubac,

If Christ is the sacrament of God, the Church is for us the sacrament of Christ; she represents him, in the full and ancient meaning of the term, she really makes him present. She not only carries on his work, but she is his very continuation, in a sense far more real than that in which it can be said that any human institution is its founder's continuation. (De Lubac 1950, 28)

The Gospels show us that some, even having encountered Christ, rejected him, and this possibility is open to all who encounter Christ through the Church. But in the respondents' stories, there are those whose experiences of the Church seem far from an encounter with Christ. In the Creed, we profess that the Church is "holy" and yet we know that, "clasping sinners to her bosom, [she is] at once holy and always in need of purification, [and] follows constantly the path of penance and renewal" (*CCC* §827; see Bullivant 2016c).

The mystery of the coexistence of holiness and sin in the Church recalls Christ's parable where weeds grew up among the wheat (Matt 13:24–30). When asked whether the weeds should be gathered, the householder replied, "Let both of them grow together until the harvest; and at harvest time I will tell the reapers, Collect the weeds first and bind them in bundles to be burned, but gather the wheat into my barn" (13:30).

To the extent that the Church has failed to be a sacramental sign of Christ, there are two ways to respond. First, to ask forgiveness. These stories help us to recognize with humility how the faith has not always been handed on effectively; how the abuse of power, infighting, and disunity have weakened faith; how the culture in some parishes has caused people to turn away; how we have failed as parishes to engage with people's doctrinal and moral doubts, or even to build up friendships within which these discussions can be aired. The anguish expressed in some of these stories should lead us to repentance for the ways we have repelled people rather than attracted them.

Second, to recall our identity as the Church. "The Church exists in order to evangelize," it is our "deepest identity" (Paul VI, *Evangelii Nuntiandi* 14). Jesus Christ summed up his mission plainly when he said, "For the Son of Man came to seek out and to save the lost" (Luke 19:10). He bestowed this same mission on the Church when he commanded us, "Go therefore and make disciples of all nations" (Matt 28:19). Sadly, sometimes we give the impression that our "deepest identity" is self-preservation. Pope Francis has warned frequently that an inward focus in the Church is like a sickness. Prior to the conclave at which he was elected pope, he wrote the following:

> When the Church does not go out of herself to evangelize, she becomes self-referential; she grows ill (like the stooped woman in the Gospel). The evils which appear throughout history in Church institutions are rooted in this self-referentiality—a kind of theological narcissism. (Quoted in Berg 2013)

His diagnosis resonates with many respondents:

> The Catholic Church really needs to change and become less of a Catholic club before I could even consider returning. (female, 68)
>
> Sometimes there appears to be more emphasis on operating procedures than [living] the gospel. (male, 45)

Ecclesial self-absorption leads us to be unconcerned with Jesus's mission, unconcerned about those who are lost. The answer to this sickness in the Church is no less than what Pope Francis has called a "missionary transformation" (*Evangelii Gaudium* 19). He calls for "a missionary option capable of transforming everything" (no. 27), so that every aspect of our parishes will be mission centered. Only in rediscovering our deepest identity can the Church once again become healthy, fulfilling her purpose of making disciples.

> May the world of our time, which is searching, sometimes with anguish, sometimes with hope, be enabled to receive the good news not from evangelizers who are dejected, discouraged, impatient or anxious, but from ministers of the Gospel whose lives glow with fervor, who have first received the joy of Christ. (Paul VI, *Evangelii Nuntiandi* 80)

PASTORAL RECOMMENDATIONS

It is impossible to address each of the issues raised in the responses. However, in this section, we follow up with practical recommendations and the proposal that a paradigm shift in parish life is needed if the Church is to be more effective both at withstanding the corrosive acids of secularism and religious indifference—which, in many ways, is the same task—at making disciples.

In his influential book *Divine Renovation*, Fr. James Mallon diagnoses and elaborates further on much of the self-referential sickness ailing our parishes. He suggests that a renewal of culture is required in many parish communities, a renewal that corresponds to Pope Francis's call for a "missionary transformation." The challenge is not small, since cultural realities within a community are subconscious; they have "gravitational" pull that shape and form us. Change, therefore, must be necessarily gradual and intentional. In chapter 5 of his book, Fr. Mallon suggests the following ten areas in which culture can slowly be shifted.

Giving Priority to the Weekend

For most Catholics, Sunday Mass is the one point of contact with their parish. The Mass is the "source and summit" of Christian life (*Lumen Gentium* 11), although for many Catholics it would seem to be "solo and sufficient"! Fr. Mallon comments that the only time 80 percent of parishioners are seen is at the weekend, and yet only 20 percent of his time was given to planning, preparing, and executing weekend Masses (Mallon 2014, 95). Given that so many respondents noted that Mass was not a life-giving experience, the investment of a parish into the experience people have when they attend Mass on a Sunday is surely invaluable. The three specific areas where an impact can be made are: hospitality, music, and homilies.

Hospitality

A sense of welcome, or lack of it, has been a constant theme through these pages:

> Friendliness is so simple, but my parish has been so unwelcoming to my children and me. (female, 37)

Reflecting on how we welcome people shifts our mentality from that of a club (that exists for its own members) to that of a church (that exists for those who do not yet belong). Hospitality is not just the job of one team who hand out hymn books, but rather the attitude of the entire parish who see themselves as hosts, not guests.

Music

Some respondents referred to their experience of Mass as "somber and joyless" and "tedious and dreary." We have already referenced how contentious an issue liturgy was. Fr. Mallon's suggestion that there is a place for both old and new in our worship is important. On the one hand, "the old must have a place in our worship, because the Church is always the Communion of Saints stretched out across history. To be Catholic is to be in the Church 'according to the whole' (*kath'holon* in Greek), and this 'whole Church' does not permit geographic or chronological limitation" (Mallon 2014, 112). Yet at the same time, the Church is missionary: "The worship of the liturgy must also have a missional dimension and must bring ancient and eternal realities to bear in a way that can be understood and received by the people who gather" (112).

Faced with the problem of a variety of musical preferences, one solution might be for liturgical planning to take place above the parish level, for example, allowing each deanery to have a dedicated Extraordinary Form of the Mass, or a Mass for those with small children, or a Mass for young adults who favor a certain musical style. This would be a better solution rather than the current status quo where each parish is pressured to cater to all over a single weekend—an impossibility—with the result that actual provision ends up being random and patchy.

Homilies

That so many respondents noted that their spiritual needs had not been met by the Church poses both a wake-up call and a huge challenge to homilists. Pope Francis's quip in *Evangelii Gaudium* rings true with many of the respondents' comments: "Both [the people] and their ordained ministers suffer because of homilies: the laity from having to listen to them and the clergy from having to preach them!" (no. 135). Yet the homily is often the only time in the week that a parishioner will receive direct teaching on the Scriptures.

> Often, the homily was short and left me wondering about the faith. Hard issues were always avoided! No deep exploration of the teachings of the Church or the Bible. (male, 27)

Many commented on how homilies and teachings they had heard did not connect with their experience of everyday life. The need for a focus on the subjective perspective in catechesis and personal accompaniment, explored earlier, can also be applied to the homily. In the West, we have been affected by a post-Enlightenment culture that dwells comfortably in the realm of ideas. And yet, to the postmodern believer, experience speaks louder than ideas; witnesses are believed over teachers.

Fr. Mallon offers several tips (Mallon 2014, 131ff.), including the importance of beginning with an attention-grabbing "hook" and knowing how you are going to "land" at the end. He places emphasis on preparation, if the preacher chooses to go "text-free": "The extra work is worth it, as our people experience that they are truly entering into a dialogue rather than listening to a monologue. Even an unpolished homily, delivered without constantly gazing at a text, is much more engaging than the most brilliant oration that is read out loud" (132). Pope Francis also devotes a section of *Evangelii Gaudium* to the homily (nos. 135–59), advising that it is "the touchstone for judging a pastor's closeness and ability to communicate to his people" (no. 135).

Meaningful Community

Respondents frequently referred to the lack of connection with others that they experienced in their parish communities:

> I was mostly left to my own devices, aside from sitting through Mass for an hour a week. I don't think most people can stay involved if that's all there is as a connection. (male, 28)
>
> I am looking for real Christian community—a 24/7 loving caring community—not just a mainly Sunday, ritual, liturgical Church. (male, 52)

In many responses, there was a desire to belong to a community in which to explore the content of belief. This desire is not accommodated by the traditional parish paradigm of "behave-believe-belong." In Fr. Mallon's words, "Are we willing to provide experiences of belonging for those who do not *yet* believe, and do not *yet* behave?" (Mallon 2014, 140). The movement toward a "belong-believe-behave" paradigm is embodied by courses such as Alpha, where people are welcomed and able to share their own thoughts, before hearing the message of the Gospel. Saint Benedict Parish, where Fr. Mallon was pastor when he wrote *Divine Renovation*, also attempts to challenge the culture of anonymity at Mass through such innovations as "Name Tag Sunday," "prayer partners at Mass," and "prayer ministry after Mass." Without undermining the integrity of the Mass itself, these customs potentially weave a greater sense of community into the celebration.

Clear Expectations

We have noted that a surprising number of respondents had joined another Christian community since leaving the Catholic Church. What is interesting is that, for many of them, their commitment to their new church is greater than what was expected of them in their Catholic parish. There can be a dangerous pressure toward minimalism in our parishes that, rather than making disciples, can, in fact, belittle the significance of faith in people's consciousness. The Gallup organization, which has created a survey to help churches measure their membership engagement (ME[25] – Member Engagement Survey), in its vast experience of working with churches, affirms the importance of expectations to organizational health. People who know what is expected of them, rather than being put off, are *more* likely to feel a sense of belonging and engagement with their parish. Saint Benedict Parish, after outlining what the parish offers to parishioners, makes clear its five expectations of all members: to worship, grow, serve, connect, and give (Mallon 2014, 156ff.)

Strength-Based Ministry

Belonging to a parish community involves service, and sometimes the parish can be like a football match: twenty-two players who need a rest from running around and being watched by twenty-two thousand who could really use some exercise. Building up a culture of leadership where everybody does something, rather than some people doing everything, is vital for the health of a parish. Not only does it involve apprenticing new people to tasks rather than doing every task yourself, but such a culture is one way of guarding against cliques that naturally arise when a limited number of volunteers in the church do everything.

People find service life-giving when they are volunteering according to their strengths. When we volunteer because of guilt or pressure, our commitment to our parish lessens rather than deepens:

> Sometimes there is nothing worse than the assumption that, as an unmarried woman, you would be willing to take on all the tea making and washing up or organize another tabletop sale. (female, 42)

Fr. Mallon writes that one of the first appointments he made at Saint Benedict was a staff member who would assist parishioners to use Gallup's StrengthsFinder test. By identifying their top five God-given strengths, parishioners are encouraged to invest in them, with the knowledge that God wants them to work through their strengths and their passions.

> I would like to see parish priests who will listen to their parishioners and work with them and not over them, using their skills, qualifications, and experience. (male, 52)

In addition to working out of their natural strengths, helping parishioners discern their supernatural charisms—the way that God channels his power and love through them for the good of others—can be life-changing. The discovery that God wants to use you in a unique way for the evangelization of the world and transformation of society is the ultimate game changer in helping Catholics become outward focused. In the Diocese of Portsmouth, hundreds of laypeople have discerned their charisms through the "Called and Gifted" discernment process, devised by the Catherine of Siena Institute (see Weddell 2012, 2015).

Formation of Small Communities

Notable in many of the responses was the overwhelming expectation people have of priests. We still operate according to a mindset where the parish priest offers personal pastoral care to each parishioner. Not only is this an impossible expectation, it also perpetuates a clerical culture where personal connection with the priest is everything.

Numerous stories from respondents detailed how they had stopped attending Mass only to find that no one followed up with them.

> Not one member of the congregation ever called, came over, or bothered to ask me why I had suddenly stopped coming. (male, 42)

In such situations, perhaps parishioners presume either the priest must be in contact with the person concerned or they do not wish to pry. From the priest's perspective, it is humanly impossible to keep tabs on hundreds of families and individuals.

In many churches, the solution to this problem has been to found small to midsize communities that meet regularly. One sixty-five-year-old woman commented,

> My current [non-Catholic] church has link groups where there are ten or fifteen of us who meet once a month and support each other and have Bible study and social time. We also use the group to volunteer and fill rotas for the church, and it stops people feeling alone and getting overlooked, especially if sick or struggling.

In today's Christian landscape, this model has been most closely identified with Evangelical megachurches. Here, large Sunday congregations are typically sustained throughout the week by a large network of much smaller meet-up groups, of all kinds, including those with a direct religious focus (prayer groups, Bible studies), and those whose *explicit* emphasis is primarily social (sports teams, parent-and-toddler sessions, coffee meet-up groups, etc.).

Such small groups are, however, by no means foreign to the British Catholic experience. Indeed, it is worth recalling the remarkable array of groups, teams, societies, sodalities, and associations that were a common feature of parish life well within living memory (see Scott 1967, 51; Harris 2013, 36). Today, it is worth considering the role that existing groups—the Catenians, the Society of Saint Vincent de Paul, the Legion of Mary—already play, and, moreover, *could*, with the right encouragement and promotion, potentially play in the future.

Regardless of how a parish organizes such communities, it is certain that many of the respondents longed for such an experience. As one thirty-four-year-old man noted: "Too many people feel lost, and the Church needs to challenge and up its game."

Experience of the Holy Spirit

One young woman (20) wrote,

> I don't see wide signs that God is working at the parish level. If Jesus Christ isn't changing hearts and transforming people, then they start to get frustrated with rules and doctrine.

Fr. Mallon comments how renewal movements in the history of the Church have always had a fresh experience of the Holy Spirit at their center, and yet amid calls for renewal, "we continue to be more comfortable with the idea of the Holy Spirit rather than the experience of the Holy Spirit who comes in power" (Mallon 2004, 182). While expressions of enthusiasm are normal at sporting events or concerts, and in the faith of those in the southern hemisphere, for Western Catholics, our cultural heritage tends to make us suspicious of expressions of spirituality that touch the emotions and write them off as "charismatic": "We are emotionally consti-pated when it comes to expressing our faith" (Mallon 2014, 185). He comments that for postmodern seekers, emotional religious experiences are not feared but welcomed. Fr. Mallon gives sugges-tions about how to make this cultural shift on a parish level, includ-ing using the Alpha programs to create an environment where people can experience the Holy Spirit, perhaps for the first time.

Becoming an Inviting Church

Finally, Fr. Mallon outlines how, for a parish to be evangeliz-ing, it needs to become more intentionally invitational. This is a shift in culture where it becomes normal to invite somebody to your parish, thus launching people from discipleship to apostleship. This requires accepting that the response to most of your invita-tions will be "no," but the more invitations, the more chance of a "yes." As Pope Francis expresses, "The drive to go forth and give, to go out from ourselves, to keep pressing forward in our sowing of the good seed, remains ever present" (*Evangelii Gaudium* 21).

CONCLUSION

It would be easy to feel overwhelmed by the stories in this book and tempting to think that the challenge before us is too colossal to undertake. With the Church's renewed emphasis on evangelization, clergy and laypeople alike can feel that their already heavy parish workload is being increased with extra tasks. The shift invites a fresh look at our pastoral endeavors, to be honest with ourselves, and ask of each parish activity, "Are we doing this because it has always been done or is this truly making disciples?" The mis-sionary transformation of our parishes requires honesty, courage, determination, and above all, a reliance on the Holy Spirit: "And remember, I am with you always, to the end of the age" (Matt 28:20).

AFTERWORD

What Must We Do?

FR. JAMES MALLON

What Must We Do? is a question that springs to the heart and mind after reading through this report from the Diocese of Portsmouth, the contents of which sound all too familiar from the other side of the Atlantic. It is a question that arises from the experience of being convicted, moved, and indeed "cut to the heart" (Acts 2:37). It is a question that not only needs to be asked but answered. Sometimes in life, including within the Church, the response to a crisis is to simply do something. Something, surely, is better than nothing, but our times require that careful attention be given to how we answer the question of how we can help fallen-away Catholics return home and prevent others from leaving. What we do must be faithful to who we are as a Church and the mission given to us by Jesus. We must avoid the temptation simply to create a plan to respond to perceived needs.

When creating any action plan, we need to ask ourselves what success looks like. This can define the parameters of a proposed solution, and when it comes to those who leave the Church for a myriad of reasons, we need to acknowledge that there never has been, and never will be, a perfect solution. There never will be a version of the Church—a parish or an expression of Catholic Christianity—that will compel no one to leave and all to return. Jesus, himself, was unable to do this. Those disciples who walked away when he spoke about the Eucharist in John 6, the rich, young man who turned away from following Jesus because the price was too high, or those who took offense at him and opposed him with ferocious hostility are reminders of the words of Jesus: "If the world hates you, be aware that it hated me before it hated you" (John 15:18).

In truth, there are some things that we cannot change and, even if we did, would likely not succeed in luring the absent back, for often, the issue is not the issue. My own experience of being a parish priest for seventeen years tells me that people will live in the tension of conflicted beliefs if they can experience real belonging. As they are loved and cared for—as they come into contact and grow in relationship with Jesus—many of the issues cease to be such. This will happen if, after loving and accompanying people, we make our primary purpose to propose the person of Jesus Christ and not to preach the Church. If we bring people through an experience of belonging to believing, then behavior will change and the Church will be embraced and eventually understood and loved.

There is nothing new here for us. This is a most traditional pastoral response coming from the mouth of Jesus himself that the world will know we are his disciples "if you have love for one another" (John 13:35). Tertullian tells us that the pagans who observe the infant Church living out their faith had the same reaction as they exclaimed, "See how they love one another" (*The Apology*, 39). It is within the web of a caring community embodied in local parishes throughout the world that we can truly accompany the weak and the broken, the perplexed and the confused, and those who are gradually opening their hearts to Christ. It cannot be an accompaniment that meanders with no goal in mind. We have a goal. It is ultimately communion with Christ and a commitment to walk the path to holiness and mission, on which each person can receive the truth that is spoken in love (see Eph 4:15).

If having genuine love, concern, and care for one another is the key that unlocks the door of faith and lived communion within the Church, then we must truly examine our motives when we ask the question "What must we do?" Any expression of outreach that is not rooted in disinterested, unconditional love of those we are attempting to reach will be ineffective. If we did not care about those who are far from Christ and his Church before we were aware of our decline, how will our efforts not be rooted in a desire for self-preservation unless there is a true change of heart? This, possibly, is the first thing we need to do. As suggested in the concluding chapter of this book, we must gather together in our dioceses and in our parishes to repent for our lukewarmness, our lack of passion, our self-referentiality, and ask God to put a new heart in us, a heart that is ready to say, "Here I am, Lord, send me" (see Isa 6:8), to the one who was himself sent, "to seek out and to save the lost" (Luke 19:10).

APPENDIX

The MyStoryShared Survey

For reference purposes, we give below the text used in the full survey. This was administered online via the interface provided by Bristol Online Surveys. As noted in the introduction, our survey design owes much to previous work by three teams of American scholars: William J. Byron and Charles Zech (Diocese of Trenton, NJ); Philip R. Hardy, Kelly L. Kandra, and Brian G. Patterson (Diocese of Springfield, IL); and Patrick J. Hornbeck and Tom Beaudoin (Fordham University, NY). A debt of gratitude is owed to the Springfield, Illinois team, whose survey design we—with permission—most closely mirrored to facilitate the possibility of cross-national comparisons.

PARTICIPANT INFORMATION AND CONSENT

Welcome to a confidential online consultation being conducted by researchers at St. Mary's University, Twickenham, in partnership with the RC Diocese of Portsmouth.

You are eligible to participate if you are (a) aged 18 years of age or older; (b) have been baptized as a Catholic; (c) either live or have lived *within the Diocese of Portsmouth* (that is, Hampshire, Berkshire, South Oxfordshire, parts of Dorset, the Isle of Wight, and the Channel Islands) and (d) no longer practise the Catholic faith (for whatever reason).

The survey is primarily intended to help inform the Diocese of Portsmouth's pastoral mission; results will also contribute to ongoing academic research into the life and experiences of baptized

Catholics in Britain. This survey should take you approximately 10 to 15 minutes to complete.

The survey is anonymous. Responses will be collected and analysed by a joint team from St. Mary's and the diocesan Social Research Unit. Any information provided by respondents that could be used to identify them (for example, references to specific people or places) will be kept confidential and will be edited out in any reports or publications arising from the study. Responses received as part of this study may be used to inform future research projects under the direction of the principal investigator.

1. I agree to participate in this research* (Required)

Yes (continue with survey).

No, I do not wish to participate.

BACKGROUND

2. Please state your sex:* (Required)

Male

Female

3. Please state your age (as of your last birthday):* (Required)

4. What is your connection to the Diocese of Portsmouth? Please choose as many or as few that apply:* (Required)

Currently live in Portsmouth Diocese

Close family connection to Portsmouth Diocese

Used to live in Portsmouth Diocese

5. Which of these groups best describes the way you think of yourself? *Please choose as many or as few as apply* (Optional)

White (Any origin)

Black (African origin)

Black (Caribbean origin)

Black (Other origin)

Asian (Indian origin)

Asian (Pakistani origin)

Asian (Bangladeshi origin)

Asian (Chinese origin)

Asian (Other origin)

Mixed origin

Other

Prefer not to say

    a. If you selected "Other," please specify.

FURTHER INFORMATION

6. Were you raised in a Catholic family?

    a. If no, at what age did you become Catholic? Please feel free to give any further details about how and why this came about.

7. Would you say that you now regard yourself to be Catholic? (for example, when asked about your religious affiliation on forms or surveys)

Yes

No

Sometimes, but not others

    a. If no or sometimes, what would be the most accurate way to describe your religious affiliation? (Optional)

No religion

Christian (no denomination)

Church of England/Anglican

Baptist

Methodist

Church of Scotland/Presbyterian

Other Christian

Jewish

Hindu

Sikh

Muslim

Buddhist

Other

i. If you selected "Other," please specify:
(Optional)

ii. If you would like to add any further comments about how you view your religious
affiliation and/or identity, please feel free
to do so here.

**8. Apart from special occasions such as weddings,
funerals and baptisms, how often nowadays do you
attend Mass?**

Once a week or more

Less often but at least once in two weeks

Less often but at least once a month

Less often but at least twice a year

Less often but at least once a year

Less often than once a year

Never or practically never

Varies too much to say

REASONS

These two questions are intended to shed light on the various journeys people take in ceasing to practise the Catholic faith, or—in some cases—no longer regarding themselves as Catholics. *There are no right or wrong answers.* You are invited simply to narrate your story, in your own words, including anything that you think is relevant.

9. **Was there a time in your life when you attended Mass on a more regular basis? Please explain what has changed between then and now.** *Feel free to give as much detail as you would like.*

10. **If you no longer regard yourself as Catholic (or only regard yourself as Catholic some of the time, but not at others), please explain how this has come about.** *Please feel free to give as much detail as you would like.*

SPECIFIC ISSUES

Next, you will have the opportunity to provide your opinion on specific factors that may have contributed to your decision to leave the Church. While some of these statements are similar to questions in the previous section, it is important that you provide us with your honest opinions so that we gain as much information as possible through this survey.

11. **For each of the statements listed below, please mark your level of agreement as a factor in your decision to stop attending Sunday Mass or leave the Catholic Church.**

a. I gradually lost interest in going to Mass.

Strongly agree

Agree

Neutral/No opinion

Disagree

Strongly disagree

b. My work schedule made it difficult to attend Mass.

Strongly agree

Agree

Neutral/No opinion

Disagree

Strongly disagree

c. My personal schedule made it difficult to attend Mass.

Strongly agree

Agree

Neutral/No opinion

Disagree

Strongly disagree

d. The priest was unfriendly.

Strongly agree

Agree

Neutral/No opinion

Disagree

Strongly disagree

e. It was difficult to understand the priest because English was his second language.

Strongly agree

Agree

Neutral/No opinion

Disagree

Strongly disagree

f. The parish staff (for example, administration, lay workers) were unfriendly.

Strongly agree

Agree

Neutral/No opinion

Disagree

Strongly disagree

g. There are too many scandals in the Catholic Church.

Strongly agree

Agree

Neutral/No opinion

Disagree

Strongly disagree

h. The parish and diocese make too many requests for money.

Strongly agree

Agree

Neutral/No opinion

Disagree

Strongly disagree

i. The parish lacks adult programmes and services (for example, specific groups or Masses aimed at adults).

Strongly agree

Agree

Neutral/No opinion

Disagree

Strongly disagree

j. The Catholic Mass is too ritualistic.

Strongly agree

Agree

Neutral/No opinion

Disagree

Strongly disagree

k. The Catholic Mass is too formal.

Strongly agree

Agree

Neutral/No opinion

Disagree

Strongly disagree

l. Music during the Catholic Mass is not enjoyable.

Strongly agree

Agree

Neutral/No opinion

Disagree

Strongly disagree

m. My parish closed, and I didn't like the new parish.

Strongly agree

Agree

Neutral/No opinion

Disagree

Strongly disagree

n. Many of my friends have left the Church.

Strongly agree

Agree

Neutral/No opinion

Disagree

Strongly disagree

o. My parish eliminated altar girls; now only boys serve.

Strongly agree

Agree

Neutral/No opinion

Disagree

Strongly disagree

p. The Latin Mass excluded my participation.

Strongly agree

Agree

Neutral/No opinion

Disagree

Strongly disagree

q. I prefer the Latin Mass but there is none in my area.

Strongly agree

Agree

Neutral/No opinion

Disagree

Strongly disagree

r. I found a religion/denomination that I like more.

Strongly agree

Agree

Neutral/No opinion

Disagree

Strongly disagree

12. **From this list of issues and policies, please select whether one or more of these was a reason for distancing yourself from the Catholic Church.**

a. Church doctrine on homosexuality

Very much

Somewhat

Neutral/no opinion

Slightly

Not at all

b. Church doctrine on abortion

Very much

Somewhat

Neutral/no opinion

Slightly

Not at all

c. Church doctrine on birth control

Very much

Somewhat

Neutral/no opinion

Slightly

Not at all

d. Church doctrine on fertility treatments

Very much

Somewhat

Neutral/no opinion

Slightly

Not at all

e. Church doctrine on divorce/remarriage

Very much

Somewhat

Neutral/no opinion

Slightly

Not at all

f. Church doctrine on the Bible

Very much

Somewhat

Neutral/no opinion

Slightly

Not at all

g. Church doctrine on women being priests

Very much

Somewhat

Neutral/no opinion

Slightly

Not at all

h. Church doctrine on marital status of priests

Very much

Somewhat

Neutral/no opinion

Slightly

Not at all

13. Please tell us if any of the statements below reflect how you feel about the Catholic Church:

a. I am dissatisfied with the atmosphere of the Catholic Mass.

Strongly agree

Agree

Neutral/No opinion

Disagree

Strongly disagree

b. I am uncomfortable with the feeling of community in my parish.

Strongly agree

Agree

Neutral/No opinion

Disagree

Strongly disagree

c. My spiritual needs were not being met.

Strongly agree

Agree

Neutral/No opinion

Disagree

Strongly disagree

d. I stopped believing in Catholic teaching.

Strongly agree

Agree

Neutral/No opinion

Disagree

Strongly disagree

ADDITIONAL INFORMATION

In this final section of the survey, you will be asked a series of questions that will allow you to type your own additional comments for many of the questions. We encourage you to take the time to provide your thoughts in the comments section following the questions.

14. Are there any religious beliefs or practices specific to the Catholic Church that trouble you?

Yes

No

a. If yes, please elaborate on your reasoning: (Optional)

15. Generally speaking, have you had a "bad experience" with any person associated with the Church?

Yes

No

a. If yes, please elaborate on your reasoning: (Optional)

16. **Can you imagine yourself returning to the Church? If so, what specific things might the Church do to help toward this?**

17. **What things do you find attractive about the Catholic Church? These can either be in general, or in the Diocese of Portsmouth specifically.**

18. **If you could communicate with the Bishop directly, what would you like to say?**

CONCLUSION

Thank you very much for your participation in this survey.

BIBLIOGRAPHY

Appiah, Kwame Anthony. "Mistaken Identities: The Reith Lectures—BBC, Radio 4." *BBC.* 2016. http://www.bbc.co.uk/programmes/b080twcz.

Beaudoin, Tom, and J. Patrick Hornbeck. "Deconversion and Ordinary Theology: A Catholic Study." In *Exploring Ordinary Theology: Everyday Christian Believing and the Church,* edited by Jeff Astley and Leslie J. Francis, 33–44. Aldershot: Ashgate, 2013.

Benedict XVI. *Light of the World: The Pope, the Church, and the Signs of the Times—A Conversation with Peter Seewald.* San Francisco: Ignatius Press, 2010.

Berg, Thomas. "*Evangelii Gaudium*: Exhorting a Self-referential Church." *Catholic News Agency.* December 5, 2013. http://www.catholicnewsagency.com/column/evangelii-gaudium-exhorting-a-self-referential-church-2753/.

Berger, Peter L. *The Sacred Canopy: Elements of a Sociological Theory of Religion.* New York: Anchor Books, [1967] 1990.

Bullivant, Stephen. (2016a) *Contemporary Catholicism in England and Wales: A Statistical Report Based on Recent British Social Attitudes Survey Data.* Catholic Research Forum Reports 1. Twickenham, London: Benedict XVI Centre for Religion and Society, 2016. http://www.stmarys.ac.uk/benedict-xvi/docs/2016-may-contemporary-catholicism-report.pdf.

———. (2016b) "Catholic Disaffiliation in Britain: A Quantitative Overview." *Journal of Contemporary Religion* 31, no. 2 (2016): 1–17.

———. (2016c) "Vatican II and Abuses in the Church: 'A community composed of men' that is 'always in need of being purified.'" In *Theology and Power: International Perspectives,* edited by S. Bullivant, D. Pilario, E. Genilo, and A. Brazal, 123–36. Mahwah, NJ: Paulist Press, 2016.

Bullivant, Stephen, and Luke Arredondo. *O My Jesus: The Meaning of the Fátima Prayer.* Mahwah, NJ: Paulist Press, 2017.

Byron, William J., and Charles Zech. "Why They Left." *America*, April 30, 2012, 17–23.

CBCEW. "Non-Churchgoing Catholics." 2017. http://www.cbcew.org .uk/CBCEW-Home/Departments/Evangelisation-and -Catechesis/Crossing-the-Threshold-Non-Churchgoing-Catholics.

Center for Applied Research in the Apostolate. "The Impact of Religious Switching and Secularization on the Estimated Size of the U.S. Adult Catholic Population." 2008. https://cara .georgetown.edu/caraservices/FRStats/Winter2008.pdf.

Congregation for the Clergy. *General Catechetical Directory*. April 11, 1971. http://www.vatican.va/roman_curia/congregations/ cclergy/documents/rc_con_cclergy_doc_11041971_gcat_en .html.

———. *General Directory for Catechesis*. August 15, 1997. http://www .vatican.va/roman_curia/congregations/cclergy/documents/rc _con_ccatheduc_doc_17041998_directory-for-catechesis_en .html.

De Lubac, Henri. *Catholicism*. London: Burns and Oates, 1950.

Diat, Nicolas, and Robert Sarah. *God or Nothing: A Conversation on Faith*. San Francisco: Ignatius Press, 2015.

Dixon, R., S. Bond, K. Engebretson, R. Rymarz, B. Cussen, and K. Wright. *Research Project on Catholics Who Have Stopped Attending Mass: Final Report*. Melbourne: Australian Catholic Bishops Conference, 2007. https://www.catholic.org.au/all-downloads/ organisations-1/pastoral-research-office-1/197-disconnected -catholics-report-april-2007-1/file.

Francis, Leslie J., and Philip J. Richter. *Gone for Good? Church Leaving and Returning in the 21st Century*. London: Epworth Press, 2007.

Hardy, Philip R., Kelly L. Kandra, and Brian G. Patterson. *Joy and Grievance in an American Diocese: Results from Online Surveys of Active and Inactive Catholics in Central Illinois*. Lisle, IL: Benedictine University, 2014. http://www.dio.org/uploads/files/Communications/ Press_Releases/2014/Joy-and-Grievance-PUBLIC-FINAL-sep-11 -2014.pdf.

Harris, Alana. *Faith in the Family: A Lived Religious History of English Catholicism, 1945–82*. Manchester: Manchester University Press, 2013.

Hoge, D. R., with K. McGuire, B. F. Stratman, and A. A. Illig. *Converts, Dropouts, Returnees: A Study of Religious Change among Catholics*. Washington, DC: USCCB; New York: Pilgrim Press, 1981.

Holy See. *Catechism of the Catholic Church.* Vatican City: Libreria Editrice Vaticana, 1994.

Hornbeck, J. Patrick. "Deconversion and Disaffiliation in Contemporary US Roman Catholicism." *Horizons* 40, no. 2 (2013): 262–74.

Hornsby-Smith, Michael P. *Roman Catholics Beliefs in England: Studies in Social Structure since the Second World War.* Cambridge: Cambridge University Press, 1987.

John Paul II. *Catechesi Tradendae.* Vatican City: Libreria Editrice Vaticana, 1979. http://w2.vatican.va/content/john-paul-ii/en/ apost_exhortations/documents/hf_jp-ii_exh_16101979 _catechesi-tradendae.html.

Mallon, James. *Divine Renovation: Bringing Your Parish from Maintenance to Mission.* New London: Twenty-Third Publications, 2014.

Martin, Ralph. *Will Many Be Saved? What Vatican II Actually Teaches and Its Implications for the New Evangelization.* Grand Rapids, MI: Eerdmans, 2012.

Packard, Joshua. "Meet the 'Dones.'" *Christianity Today* (Summer 2015). http://www.christianitytoday.com/pastors/2015/summer -2015/meet-dones.html.

Packard, Josh, and Ashleigh Hope. *Church Refugees: Sociologists Reveal Why People Are Done with Church but Not Their Faith.* Loveland, CO: Group Publishing, 2015.

Paul VI. *Evangelii Nuntiandi.* Vatican City: Libreria Editrice Vaticana, 1975. http://w2.vatican.va/content/paul-vi/en/apost_exhortations/ documents/hf_p-vi_exh_19751208_evangelii-nuntiandi.html.

Pew Research Center. *Faith in Flux: Changes in Religious Affiliation in the U.S.* April 27, 2009. http://www.pewforum.org/files/2009/04/ fullreport.pdf.

———. *U.S. Catholics Open to Non-Traditional Families: 45% of Americans Are Catholics or Connected to Catholicism.* September 2, 2015. http:// www.pewforum.org/files/2015/09/Catholics-and-Family-Life-09 -01-2015.pdf.

Pontifical Council for Culture. *The* Via Pulchritudinis: *Privileged Pathway for Evangelisation and Dialogue.* Vatican City: Libreria Editrice Vaticana, 2006. http://www.vatican.va/roman_curia/ pontifical_councils/cultr/documents/rc_pc_cultr_doc _20060327_plenary-assembly_final-document_en.html.

Pope Francis. *Evangelii Gaudium.* Vatican City: Libreria Editrice Vaticana, 2013. http://w2.vatican.va/content/francesco/en/

apost_exhortations/documents/papa-francesco_esortazione-ap_20131124_evangelii-gaudium.html.

Ratzinger, Joseph. *Milestones: Memoirs 1927-1977.* San Francisco: Ignatius Press, 1998.

———. "Address to Catechists and Religion Teachers." Jubilee of Catechists. December 12, 2000. https://www.ewtn.com/new_evangelization/ratzinger.htm.

Richter, Philip J., and Leslie J. Francis. *Gone but Not Forgotten: Church Leaving and Returning.* London: Darton, Longman & Todd, 1998.

Sarah, Robert. "Address on the 10th Anniversary of 'Summorum Pontificum.'" *The Catholic World Report,* March 31, 2017. http://www.catholicworldreport.com/Item/5532/Cardinal_Sarahs_Address_on_10th_Anniversary_of_Summorum_Pontificum.aspx.

Schmitz, Matthew. "Has Pope Francis Failed?" *New York Times,* September 28, 2016. https://www.nytimes.com/2016/09/28/opinion/has-pope-francis-failed.html.

Scott, George. *The R.C.s: A Report on Catholics in Britain Today.* London: Hutchinson, 1967.

Smith, C., K. Longest, J. Hill, and K. Christofferson. *Young Catholic America: Emerging Adults In, Out of, and Gone from the Church.* Oxford: Oxford University Press, 2014.

Smith, William G. "Does Gender Influence Online Survey Participation? A Record-linkage Analysis of University Faculty Online Survey Response Behavior." June 2008. https://eric.ed.gov/?id=ED501717.

Streib, H., R. W. Hood, B. Keller, R.-M. Csöff, and C. F. Silver. *Deconversion: Qualitative and Quantitative Results from Cross-Cultural Research in Germany and the United States of America.* Göttingen: Vandenhoeck & Ruprecht, 2009.

Taylor, Charles. *Sources of the Self: The Making of the Modern Identity.* Cambridge: Cambridge University Press, 1989.

———. *A Secular Age.* Cambridge: Harvard University Press, 2007.

Trzebiatowska, Marta, and Steve Bruce. *Why Are Women More Religious than Men?* Oxford: Oxford University Press, 2012.

Weddell, Sherry A. *Forming Intentional Disciples: The Path to Knowing and Following Jesus.* Huntington, IN: Our Sunday Visitor, 2012.

———, ed. *Becoming a Parish of Intentional Disciples.* Huntington, IN: Our Sunday Visitor, 2015.